Adventuring
in the
Spirit

BOB WHITAKER

This story is taken from my journals, diaries, correspondence,
newspaper articles and court documents. Certain names in illustrations
have been changed to protect the privacy of the individual.

ISBN: 978-1-4834-3557-2 (sc)
ISBN: 978-1-4834-3556-5 (e)

Lulu Publishing Services rev. date: 08/20/2015

"... whoever drinks of the water that I shall give will never thirst; the water that I shall give him will become in him a spring of water welling up to eternal life." John 4:14

I dedicate this story to my children: Emily, Laura, Philip, Amy & Sam; my grandchildren: Andrew, Daniel, Timothy, Casey, Patrick, Brendan, Connor, Chad, Coby and Shannon; my great-grandchildren present and future; and my friends, that they may believe and continue to receive all that the Father promises and be equipped to bring the same to others. I want to thank my wife for typing and editing this manuscript.

CONTENTS

CHAPTER 1

In the Upper Room

I grew up during the 1930s in a little town, Wyncote, PA just 15 miles north of the City Hall of Philadelphia. I had two older sisters and one younger sister. Our home was a little different from many in that my father went to church, but my mother normally did not. I remember well every Sunday he took us to Sunday school and I can picture that walk of about half a mile. After Sunday school we went home (we did not stay for worship) and mother had a delicious dinner ready for us. I believed in Jesus, that He was the Son of God, but I did not know Him as my Savior and Lord. Most of the time I was a fairly good boy but I had a terrible temper. When I would yell, the neighborhood could hear it.

When I was 18 years old I went to Haverford College, a small Quaker men's school west of Philadelphia on what is known as the Main Line. Every Thursday the whole college, some 400, attended Quaker Meeting where we sat in silence and waited for God to move somebody to speak. Some of my friends were bored with this, but I felt it was important.

I was pretty restless and wanting to have fun and during my first year I was running to and fro with dates, movies and parties. For about nine months I was very involved with a charming young woman. We were crazy in love and rebelling against parental standards. Then suddenly, I went to answer the dorm phone one day and collapsed. We were all shocked to learn that at age 19 I had a serious case of rheumatoid arthritis! I felt like my whole body was a dull toothache. One doctor said I should probably choose a sedentary occupation because it was likely I would spend much of my life in bed or a wheelchair!

This scared me to death; I began to listen to Christian radio preaching, desperately seeking answers. I soon had plenty of time. My right knee swelled up so badly that Dr. Mayock thought it best to drain the knee, immobilize the leg in a cast and put me in bed for a summer. (It was Philadelphia heat and humidity at its worst.) This sabotaged the relationship with my girl; I hated to lose her but I knew it had to be. Then I was on gold therapy and ACTH[1] for the rest of college and supposed to take it easy.

Happily, my morale recovered when I rediscovered Marilyn, the girl I had pined over in junior high, and began a delightful relationship. I took a course on the history and philosophy of Quakerism where I read the story of George Fox (1624-1691) the founder of the Quaker religion. This man was full of the Holy Spirit of God. He was a prophet in word and deed and remarkable miracles and works of mercy and justice came from his ministry. The more I read him and other

---

[1] No medical people ever inquired about the possible emotional and moral causes of my descent into arthritis.

Quakers, the more I wanted what they had. After that course I tried to live the Christian life, as I understood it, but unfortunately the harder I tried the more I looked down on my friends who weren't trying. So then I would take a week off from trying to be a good Christian.

In my senior year, one Friday night after dinner, George Coleman (a graduate of Haverford) and some of his friends from Princeton Seminary circulated in our college dining room. They announced to each table they had come to share with us what Jesus Christ meant to them personally. They said they would be upstairs in the common room to meet with any of us who cared to listen. I was fascinated. I had never heard anything like this before. I determined to go. I suppose a couple of handfuls of guys turned out to meet with these five young men. What struck me about them was their obvious love for one another, their enjoyment of each other's company, and their ability to put everybody at ease and talk with a sense of humor as well as sincerity. In other words, they were not the pious type. Their faith was down to earth and delightful. One by one they gave their testimony about how Jesus had changed their life. I was deeply touched by what they were saying. I thought, *"This is wonderful. Everybody's got to hear this."* They told us at the end they would return Sunday night and encouraged us to invite our friends to come out. Though I was busy with classes and studies most of Saturday, Saturday night and Sunday I went door knocking and, along with others, invited as many guys as I could to the Sunday night meeting.

Sunday night as we gathered, it was wonderful to see 50 or more guys show up. That night the Princetonians told different aspects of their stories; especially memorable were Ren Jackson, who was from a family of Presbyterian ministers, and Neil Hamilton who later became a seminary professor. As Neil spoke, he simply retold the story of Jesus with a focus on why and how He died. As he retold the story of the crucifixion, I was totally engrossed. In my mind's eye I could see Jesus dying on the Cross. The words of the old hymn, (The Old Rugged Cross), "The dearest and best for a world of lost sinners was slain," went through my mind and I felt myself utterly convicted of sin. There I was a selfish, inconsistent college boy looking for pleasure and kicks in life and there was the Savior sacrificially giving His life for me. Within myself I felt cast down before Him prostrate and then I felt myself lifted up in exultation before Him. I was stunned and I was captivated.

After the meeting the Princeton boys gathered with nine of us who had been touched by their message and encouraged us to share together, each in turn, what had happened to us and to pray for one another. Then they told us they hoped we would continue to meet together regularly. We decided we would meet first thing every morning for about 15 minutes.

The next morning when I woke up, though it was November 12th, it seemed like Spring; the world was new and beautiful and the birds were singing for the first time and everything was alive with life. Immediately we gathered together in what we called our "cell group." Again we shared what was happening to us and prayed for one another to live out what God was pouring in. I did not know then that I had been "born again." All I knew was Christ was alive and real to me for the first time and I felt I belonged to Him and wanted to live for Him and follow Him.

For a while we met every morning. Before long there were some 25 young men meeting in small cell groups frequently and we were sharing scriptures and experiences and encouraging one another to live for Christ. As I recall I was the chief encourager of these meetings and certainly I was benefiting enormously. Our mentors advised us to take "moral inventory" of our lives by measuring ourselves by the Sermon on the Mount and sharing our failures and weaknesses with the group, who would then pray for us. Some of those meetings were powerful with the presence of God and I felt a love for the guys I had never known before. Fortunately at that same time, the Rev. Bryan Greene from England was in Philadelphia holding evangelistic meetings and he was led to extend his meetings to Bryn Mawr College, which was nearby. Many of us went to those meetings and we were greatly edified. I can still hear him say in his inimitable way, "Jesus is Ultimate Demand and Final Succor." My girlfriend, Marilyn, also attended those meetings with us.

My mentors from Princeton wanted us all to go to New York to meet with their mentor, The Rev. Dr. Sam Shoemaker. He regularly held meetings at Calvary Episcopal Church to encourage the young men who were being reached by the Princeton group as they evangelized colleges in the northeast as they had done at Haverford. I was the only one who went. I hitchhiked to New York and there I attended some wonderful meetings led by Sam Shoemaker, Irving Harris and Dr. John Oliver Nelson (from Yale Divinity School). These men made the person of Christ enormously attractive. The atmosphere of love, joy and faith was contagious. I had never seen the likes in a church. They were concerned to make sure we not only believed in Christ, but also were totally committed to Him.

This is how they put it to me. "Is there anything you would be unwilling to do for God in the name of Jesus Christ?" My first response was, *"I'd be willing to do whatever He wants me to do."* But on closer questioning, I had to wrestle mightily. They said, "What if He wants you to be a minister?" That caused me to pause because I was not willing. My childhood minister was not someone I wanted to follow. He was brilliant but odd and I'm ashamed to say I often imitated him to the entertainment of my sisters. I thought to myself, *"To prepare a sermon every week would be like writing an English theme weekly. I would hate to do that."* So I argued with them about being a minister and their response was, "Can't you believe if God wants this He could give you the ability to do it happily?" I granted them possibly He could, but I certainly hoped he didn't want me to. Then they asked, "Would you be willing to become a missionary for the Lord?" That really stumped me. I was terrible at foreign languages; I had barely gotten through Latin and did poorly in Spanish. And I didn't want to go anywhere where I couldn't have my mother's chocolate cake and rice pudding. The thought of going to darkest Africa was frightening. So I said, *"Surely God would not want me to do that,"* and they said, "But if He did, could you trust Him and go?" And then they asked the clincher. "Would you be willing to give up your Unitarian girlfriend?" That really got me. I had known her since childhood. I had fallen in love with her in Jr. High. I had waited for her to fall in love with me for five years. They reasoned, "Can't you believe if God wants you to give her up, there are other young women who you could love as much?"

So I had a lot to wrestle with and finally I realized God did love me, He wanted what was best for me, and in the long run whatever He wanted would be the very best. So I surrendered and prayed with my newfound spiritual mentors and surrendered all to God and committed my life unreservedly to follow Jesus Christ.

At the end of that weekend, I went with Ren, Bill Cohea, Bruce Larson and company to a party somewhere in New York City. I witnessed something remarkable. They turned the party into a time of personal witness and it ended when most of the people there were involved in prayer.

It was not long before my Princeton mentors contacted me and invited me to go with them and other collegians to visit and evangelize Harvard University. I was so excited. I don't remember how I got there, but it was so worth it. Harvard is a beautiful university in Boston, MA. It was, I believe, the first American university to train men for the ministry and for the practice of law. Of course, it has come a long way from those days. We did there what my Princeton friends had done at Haverford. They secured a place where we could hold our meetings. We started each morning with wonderful times of prayer and fellowship. Then we fanned out, two by two, knocked on the doors of the dormitories to invite men to come hear the Good News about Jesus Christ. Of course we met with lots of turndowns and some sneering, but we had wonderful times and there were young men who came to Christ. During the winter of 1952 I also went with them to Princeton, to one of the women's colleges in New England and finally to Westminster College near Pittsburgh. I still remember the time in late February when we were coming back from Westminster on the Pennsylvania turnpike in a snowstorm. We shouldn't have been driving, but we needed to get back for classes Monday morning. I was taking my turn driving Ren Jackson's '36 Ford and while I was trying to see through the windshield and stay on the road, Ren asked me, "Whit, have you ever considered becoming a minister?" It was amazing, but it was as though God spoke to me and said, "**This is what you will do.**"[2] I never doubted that moment. I would be a minister of Jesus Christ; I was called. It was the most certain fact of my life.

It wasn't long before I shared excitedly with my parents that God was calling me to the ministry. Like everyone else, they were bowled over. That had not been my trajectory. They reminded me, "Bobby you have changed your major three times. We have seen you go through a number of enthusiasms, your life has not been consistent with such a calling, and how can you be sure so soon this is it?" But I kept talking over several weeks and maybe months and finally they told me they would back me and help me go to seminary and prepare for the ministry. I think the deal was, they would cover tuition and I would cover room and board.

Thanks be to God forever and ever, my rheumatoid arthritis disappeared. I don't remember the details about how fast -- it just went. In my late 20's and my 30's it tried to come back, but by the power of God I ran it off!

---

[2] See Appendix A, "Hearing God."

CHAPTER 2

Preparations

The winter and spring of 1952 was crunch time for me. I had to get everything done in order to graduate with a major in Biology by June. I was trying to do all my homework, including many papers, and somehow find time to consume the Old Testament as well as the New Testament and to make applications to seminaries. My mentors wanted me to go to Princeton. I visited there and helped them to evangelize at the university. My new Pastor wanted me to go to Yale. So I even found time to hitchhike to New Haven, CT and to meet with dear John Nelson and, though registrations were closed, he got me accepted.

The most important thing for me in the winter of '52 was time with Marilyn and time to help her come to faith in Jesus Christ and be born of the Spirit. Naturally I prayed for her, took her to meetings and spent many hours in dialogue with her about the Christian faith. In terms of her loving and patient disposition, and her ability to bring out the best in people, she was way ahead of me. By the Grace of God and with the help of a young Methodist pastor,

Tommy Ogden, she embraced Jesus as her Lord and Savior. She was hoping we could marry soon after we graduated from college, but I was not ready emotionally and felt we couldn't do that and afford for me to attend seminary. In those days seminarians were expected to be like monks and only a few had begun to get married before entering seminary. Privately, I was struggling with the warnings of my mentors. They had said I should be very careful not to marry a girl until I was sure she loved the ministry as well as she loved me.

Just before she graduated from Drexel University, Marilyn was able to get a job through the Presbyterian Board of National Missions teaching Home Economics at a mission school (Menaul) in Albuquerque, NM. She flew away while I worked building houses and setting aside money for seminary. At the end of the summer I sold my beloved '34 Ford three-window coupe.

Yale Divinity School has beautiful brick colonial buildings on lovely grounds just up Prospect Street from Yale University. Our opening meeting as students was with Dean Liston Pope. He had just finished a cigarette and greeted us coolly. He let us know right off this seminary was not a continuous revival, but would be a rigorous intellectual and emotional grind. I was shocked and put off. Nevertheless, I found that though the courses were demanding, they were interesting and I did well.

I began to miss Marilyn terribly. Even more so when I learned she was getting more and more interested in a young man at Menaul who was the son of a minister. After awhile I got alarmed and I got ready to fly to New Mexico at Christmas break and propose marriage. I cannot figure how I was able to afford an engagement ring or the flight, but I well remember leaving Philadelphia on Christmas day (I think it was snowing) and flying on a 4-engine Constellation and landing in beautiful Los Angeles in the sunlight at mid-day. In a memorable reunion we met downtown, then went to stay at her sister's home on the UCLA campus. It was there, and Santa Monica, where we courted for a few days and became engaged. Then we went back to Menaul School for about a week before I had to return to New Haven. It killed me to leave, not only Marilyn, but also the enchanting southwest. We told ourselves someday we had to come back for good. Thank God it was only six more months and we were married on June 1st back in Pennsylvania. We then spent a memorable first summer in Albuquerque while Marilyn finished teaching and I worked in a ministry to poor boys at the Martineztown Community Center. I will never forget those ragged little boys who were so poor and malnourished. It was there the Lord gave me a heart for the poor.

In late August we bought an old Nash coupe and in September we drove and camped across the U.S. and returned to New Haven. By the time we got there we had no money and were just about out of food. Our first night we slept on the lawn of Yale Divinity School. Fortunately Marilyn had landed a job teaching Home Economics and English at Hamden High School. In that way she put me through seminary. I frantically searched for a part-time job and for a few weeks worked as a sitter for a mentally ill man. I was able to persuade Mary Clemente to let us stay in her second floor apartment for a month until we could pay her rent. She was a wonderful landlady and taught Marilyn how to cook Italian.

Sometime during my second year at seminary I came to a crisis of faith. Many of our professors had a critical view of scripture; they could not accept the supernatural. They thought the miracles were exaggerated reports of the evangelists. They felt angels and demons probably did not exist and denied the healings and raisings of the dead. For example, in a course on Acts our professor told us, "Now gentlemen, here we have a delightful story by Luke. Of course it didn't happen that the Holy Spirit fell on the disciples and they spoke in some sixteen different languages, but rather this was Luke's way of saying the Gospel is intended for all nations and all peoples everywhere." Immediately hands went up. One student asked, "What about those people who claim to speak in tongues today?" As I recall, the professor explained, "Well we all know there are people who are highly suggestible emotional types who in their simplistic belief think this story is fact. Under the strong pressure of a revival meeting, they work themselves up into some sort of hysteria. Then they go off in some babbling and convince themselves it is a repeated miracle." He also suggested we find these people in economically depressed areas where people are ignorant and preyed upon by Pentecostal preachers. There were others who raised questions and I, myself, was not convinced by the professor's teaching.

One day I came home to our apartment across the street from the County Jail. I climbed up the stairs to the second floor, went in and sat down at the kitchen table and starting crying and crying. I was groaning,

"What am I supposed to believe?" Marilyn was alarmed; she feared I was losing it. We talked and prayed it out and the peace of God came. He impressed upon me I was to preach and teach the things I was sure about and pray for more light. I didn't want to leave Yale. I had a wonderful part-time ministry to college students at the downtown Presbyterian Church. We loved them and God was using us for their benefit. Also I felt if I could cope with my agnostic professors I could cope with anybody in my ministry.

When I graduated from seminary in 1955 I was confident God would give me more light and my doubts would be answered.

CHAPTER 3

Warming Up

After seminary, my first church was among the hillbillies in the mountains of Tennessee in a little community called Allardt. We loved it there and soon after we arrived our first child Emily Ann was born the day after Christmas. We never lacked for babysitters. Our people vied with one another to keep her. There, God's promise began to come true; He gave me more light. Mountain religion and mountain preachers were a challenge to me. They knew the whole Bible cover to cover and preached powerfully and compellingly. I went to their meetings and was convicted. I became acquainted with mourners' benches and foot washing. I got in touch with an awesome God. Reading Dwight Moody, the great late-19th century evangelist, nourished me. My men taught me to hunt and fish. It was an incredible adventure. I've never gotten over the mystery of a man hunting with a dog. The farm and community life was so good and the response of men and youth to our ministry was so heartening.

I saw a lot of suffering among the poor and was burdened about this. Lottie Johns, mother of fourteen children, was very sick with a chronic ear infection. For over a year, despite three hospitalizations and antibiotics, she was so dizzy and tormented with headaches and nausea, she had to lie down most of the time. I couldn't stand to see her suffer. I began to study the healing ministry of Jesus and the Apostles. It seemed to me we ought to be able to pray for the sick and see more results. I obtained literature written by denominational pastors who had made progress in praying for the sick. It was encouraging. Then I remembered how one of my professors had said, "Don't ever suppose you can do like Oral Roberts. You can't. If you tell people the prayer of faith will make them whole, you will fail and undermine their faith." **"Whoever causes one of these little ones ... to sin, it would be better for him if a great millstone were hung around his neck and he were thrown into the sea."** Mark 9:42.

Finally I screwed up my courage and went to her little farmhouse. I read stories of Jesus' healing all manner of sickness. I asked if she believed the Lord could heal her; she said she did. I said God wills to heal the whole person, but He does it in His own time and way. I encouraged her to read the Gospels to encourage her faith and to regularly confess her sins and give thanks. Then I explained I would lay hands on her and pray. She managed to get up and sit in an old wicker chair. I stood in back of the chair, put my hands over her ears, and prayed with thanksgiving and fervent petition that as Jesus once healed the sick in Galilee He would now heal in Allardt. I was too scared to ask what was happening, so I said goodbye and left quickly. Soon after, I went on vacation and when I returned I went to see Lottie. She was happy, ironing her clothes, and had a hearing aid on. She told me after I left she started to feel better; the fear and worry was replaced by a calm confidence. She told her children the Lord was healing her. The headaches and dizziness disappeared and her doctor was amazed to find the infection gone. She gave God all the praise and shared her story with friends and family. The light was increasing for me.

Although we were deeply involved in Allardt, Marilyn was sick a lot with asthma and bronchitis due to the rainy climate. Unfortunately, our prayers were not effective in her case; she got pneumonia. Finally, I got a call to a church in the Valley of the Sun, Arizona. It was heart wrenching for us to leave our little mountain church. In the next few years we would return twice to visit.

In January 1958 we drove into southern Arizona and came up through the endless acres of irrigated fields. It felt like paradise after the cold, rainy weather of the mountains. We were excited to get started as the new minister of First Presbyterian Church of Chandler, AZ. All through the winter the weather was lovely -- then the furnace came in May. On June 25th we were thrilled for Marilyn to bring forth a healthy baby girl, Laura Lynn. Sixteen months later Philip Chase joined our growing family. I always called him and Laura "two peas in a pod" they looked so much alike. And 'lo and behold, twelve months later along came Amy Sue. My parents were shocked and my Uncle Howard said, "Bobby is spending too much time at home." Which was not true, because I was very busy seeking to revive a church that had stalled.

In early 1962 I received a letter from my old friend Frank Turnball from Tennessee. Frank had been the neighboring pastor when we were in Allardt, TN. He lived in the most forlorn old coalmining town I'd ever seen. When the mine played out, everyone who could had left town, leaving behind the weak, the sick and the discouraged. Yet Frank was reporting he had received a wonderful baptism of the Holy Spirit. He and his wife Ellen were praising the Lord, enjoying His love and were full of joy unspeakable and hope. I thought surely he had taken leave of his senses, or perhaps a miracle had happened. He urged me to let him put me on the mailing list of David duPlessis. David was a South African Dutchman who had the boldness to get himself invited to meetings of the World and National Councils of Churches and other conferences. He would testify to the ministers the wonders of being baptized in the Holy Spirit and speaking in tongues.[3] Many ministers, ultimately at least 10% of the ministers of the major denominations in America, responded and received the promised blessing. They were coming together around the country to share their experiences and encourage one another to renew the denominations in the Holy Spirit.

As I read duPlessis' letters it was mind blowing. I thought at first he must have been exaggerating because his reports sounded like the Book of Acts all over again. But I began to re-read Acts and seek the Lord afresh for more of His reality.

My friend Bruce (a Presbyterian minister) told me about the gatherings of the Full Gospel Businessmen's

---

[3] See *"A Man Called Mr. Pentecost – David duPlessis"* as told to Bob Slosser.

Fellowship International (FGBFI). In the late 1950's, and throughout the '60s and '70s, led by Demos Shakarian, they would rent a huge motel with banquet room and bring in an array of inspiring speakers from all over the United States, plus worship leaders. We went several times to the Ramada Inn in Phoenix to find out what was going on. For several days their services would begin with breakfast or dinner. They struck me indelibly – men everywhere were hugging men with joyous greetings; I had never seen that before. My father said it was sissy for men to hug or kiss, so he did neither, until I initiated it in his old age. To have a big, gregarious Armenian businessman give me a bear hug nearly scared me to death! But it was great for my starched and ironed Presbyterian soul. Those men were the ones who first brought all kinds of hungry denominational seekers together and gave them a taste of Pentecostal glory. The worship with uplifted hands (which also scared me at first), led by gifted musicians, featured devotional Jesus-centered choruses that gave an intimacy with God that made me crave more. It was not uncommon for the worship to go on for an hour before a speaker was put on.

The one speaker Bruce wanted me to hear was the Rev. James Brown from an old historic Presbyterian church in southeastern Pennsylvania. The man astounded me. He was full of joy and love and it was authentic. He would get so caught up in talking about the goodness of God in Christ he would dance in the Spirit to the delight of everyone in the hall. This was not according to Presbyterian order! But it certainly reminded me of David bringing up the Ark to Jerusalem. I found out Jim had a huge Saturday night prayer meeting at his Presbyterian church every week where he led the praises with cymbals! One of his women members complained about these revival prayer meetings that brought people from all over the countryside and asked Jim, "Who is the Chairman of the Committee on Ministerial Relations in our presbytery?" She wanted to press her concern with the overseers. Whereupon Jim told her, "I am the Chairman of the Committee."[4] He was a lovely man, full of the light of Christ and his messages on the sovereignty of God were transporting.

At the Full Gospel meetings, after the featured speaker, there would be a strong invitation to salvation or prayer for the baptism of the Holy Spirit. Anyone who went forward or stood for prayer would have plenty of people ready to pray for them until something memorable would happen! I watched with considerable interest, but I wasn't quite ready to jump in.

There were other memorable speakers. One of them was John Osteen (the father of Joel). John had been a Southern Baptist but he was filled with the Holy Spirit and spoke in tongues and was given the right foot of fellowship by his denomination. He was a man full of faith; his faith was contagious. I followed reports of him over the years and incredible mighty works followed his ministry.

Another man who made a huge impression on me was William Branham. He was an incredible prophet and healer. I've never heard or seen the likes of him. He always stayed with a Presbyterian elder friend of

---

[4] When retelling this story, Jim would always break out laughing at length – it was infectious – the whole assembly would be convulsed with laughter.

mine named Carl Williams. He would pray three or four hours before he would speak. His messages would go on for at least an hour or two. It would all be an intense exposition of scripture running from Genesis to Revelation. No one was ever bored. The anointing on his words was awesome, especially so because I knew he had been raised in poverty in Kentucky, never got beyond the eighth grade, and was biblically self-taught. After the time of teaching he would go into a time of ministry. He would see a light or a vision over the heads of the people to whom he would minister. He would point to the person and say to them words like, "You, sir (or maam), the light breaks over you, the Lord has heard your prayer. Come forward for ministry." As they came close to him he would often tell them their name and why they were there. Or he would say, "If I tell you your name and why you are here will you believe that Jesus heals you now of your condition?" Then, as I recall, they would be healed without him touching them. It was through the spoken word, and quite often they would fall down under the power of the Holy Spirit. Branham was controversial and unorthodox in some of his interpretations of scripture but whenever I heard him I trembled under the power of the Holy Spirit and I knew, *"Surely, the Lord God is in this place and has spoken as of old."*

After the morning breakfast service and/or after lunch the Businessmen's meetings would feature wonderful seminars. The teachers were superb. For me the most memorable was Derek Prince. He was an Englishman with an Oxfordian accent and a Greek scholar. His testimony about being filled with the Holy Spirit while he was a British soldier was marvelous and given with a tremendous sense of humor. He was the finest Bible teacher I have ever heard. He was able to take the most demanding passages and expound on them in such a way that you went away convinced nothing could compare with the breadth and depth and riches of God's Word. Derek was also great at ministering to people in prayer and in later years became quite a leader in intercessory prayer for Israel.

CHAPTER 4

Outpouring of the Holy Spirit

Before long I heard that David duPlessis would be speaking at a free ministerial breakfast meeting at the Phoenix YMCA. I had to go. Some of my fellow Presbyterian ministers also went. We loved what we heard. I went to several other meetings where duPlessis spoke. On October 11, 1962 I went to a Thursday morning prayer meeting at the First Assembly of God Church. I was amazed to see at least 100 people gathered there. I sat next to my friend Bruce in the back and listened while David told about an Episcopal minister having his life and ministry transformed by the power of the Holy Spirit. As I listened, something was welling up within me. My heart began to pound; it got so loud I thought surely the people around me could hear it. I felt like a barrel filling up with pulsating liquid dynamite; I thought, *"If this keeps up I'm going to burst."* Then I got alarmed; *"This power is going to cause me to explode; if I don't get relief I'm going to make an emotional scene."* What was I to do? I nudged Bruce *"I can't take this anymore."* I had feared someone would see me coming to these meetings. I had feared making a spectacle of myself;[5] but the awesome power within made me not care any more; I had to ask for prayer. I raised my hand; duPlessis stopped in mid-sentence; he could see I was in distress. He said, "Yes, brother?" *"I'm sorry to interrupt, but I need you to pray for me right now."* He said, "You come on down here and we'll pray for you." Immediately the whole assembly was murmuring in prayer like the sound of many waters. duPlessis laid hands on me and began to pray fervently for me to be released in the Holy Spirit. I thought heaven's cascading torrents would cause me to speak in tongues, and I was willing, but instead I wept and then peace came over me. David said to me, "Now brother, the Lord is dealing with you. Get alone with Him and your Bible and seek His face and He will meet you."

I did what David said. Then, on Tuesday night, October 23rd, one of my new minister friends took me to an "early church" house meeting. We entered a small, 3-bedroom house in north Phoenix. All of the furniture was pushed out on the patio. Doors and windows were open and it was wall-to-wall people sitting on the floor. In the middle of the room was Jim Swink, a body and fender repairman. He welcomed all of us in the Name of Jesus. We were mostly denominational people from many different churches. A few were from his Pentecostal church. He said, "I am not the leader of this meeting, the Lord is in charge and we are to do what He prompts us to do by the Holy Spirit. He will lead different ones to read scripture and speak the Word. He will lead others to prophesy, to exhort, to bless. He will lead us in prayer. Some will speak in tongues

---

[5] The one thing a Presbyterian doesn't want to do is make a scene.

23

some will interpret. Let Him have His way with you. Do whatever He prompts you to do. Stay humble before Him and let His love rule over all." I then saw a meeting conducted by the Holy Spirit. I saw all the gifts of the Holy Spirit in operation (as listed in 1 Corinthians 12). The sense of the Presence was tremendous. I heard a couple of prophecies that sounded like something out of Isaiah. Then after about three hours, someone said, "Let's pray for the ministers of the Phoenix area." There were wonderful prayers. Finally I said, *"Well, you might as well pray for me,"* and they all gathered around and laid hands on me. I was engulfed in love. At last, in a humble place, I saw, "Glory in the church." I knew then clearly, we must not only have the preaching and hearing of the Word, the faithful administration of the sacraments and good order, but we must prayerfully seek for fullness of life in the Spirit.

I didn't get home until 2:00 AM. My family was asleep. I slipped into bed next to Marilyn. At 5:00 AM I awoke completely refreshed. I could not believe it. I went down to my study to pray and two or three hours went by. It was like that until Thursday night, October 25th when I got a tape by Dennis Bennett[6]. I had a committee meeting until 9:30 PM then went home to listen to the tape, alone in my living room. Dennis' background was like mine except he was an Episcopal priest. As he told the story of being baptized in the Holy Spirit and how his church was transformed, the room was charged with the Presence of God. It seemed as if the Risen Jesus was with me. As I walked around quietly praising the Lord, on the inside I felt like I was a well and deep down inside a spring of water was

---

[6] See Appendix B for more about this apostle of the Holy Spirit.

24

bubbling up[7] and it kept bubbling right up into my throat and words began to form and I started quietly praying in a language I had never heard. I was so full and so happy with the power and love I wanted to pray forever. I said to the Lord, *"Don't let me stop."* It was joy unspeakable and full of glory and praise. Somewhere around 11:30 I simmered down. My first thought was, *"They were wrong!"*[8] There was no hysteria, no crowd pressure. There was no out of control emotionalism. This was the most real and glorious experience I had ever had of the Lord and it was so lovely, so joyous and so peaceful.

Those late October days were times of fullness – the Everlasting spring of life kept welling up within me with joy and love. I could not get enough of prayer and scripture; the Presence of Jesus was so real. I was loving people more and wanting to bless them. For the first time in my life I felt fully equipped, ready for anything and more than ever wanting to pray for the healing of people who were sick or hurting. People started saying to me, "You are preaching more powerfully than we've ever heard you. What happened to you?" One by one I began to share with them what had happened, or I gave them a book to read like David Wilkerson's "The Cross and The Switchblade," or Catherine Marshall's "Something More." Little by little some of my leaders and members received the filling of the Holy Spirit.

About seven weeks after "the fullness" I awoke at 3:30 AM unable to sleep. I sensed the closeness of the

---

[7] "Whoever drinks of the water that I shall give him will never thirst; the water that I shall give him will become in him a spring of water welling up to eternal life." John 4:14

[8] My professors back at Yale who doubted tongues and miracles.

25

Lord. It seemed as if He was wrapping me round and round with a cloth band. Then He pulled the band tight and I felt bound secure in the Spirit. I could hear the still small voice saying, **"Get up, get up."** I argued, *"Lord if I get up now I'll be worn out in the morning and won't be able to do my work."* But He insisted, **"Get up."** So I got up and went into the living room for prayer. I no sooner sat down than it seemed I was having a powerful vision of an attractive woman in my church beckoning me to become intimate with her. I was being overwhelmed with lust. Fortunately I remembered what the Pentecostals had told me. I whispered self-consciously, *"Leave me in the Name of Jesus."* The vision weakened, so I said a bit stronger, *"Be gone in the Name of Jesus,"* and it weakened even more; finally I said, *"By the power of the blood of Jesus I command you to leave,"* and it was as though a large vacuum cleaner was turned on, the vision was sucked out of the room and I was free and praised the Lord. This was an awesome revelation of the reality of the devil and an even greater realization of the power of Jesus' name. Once again, the Lord had shown me convincingly what the scriptures teach about Satan and his demons and the power of deliverance prayer was absolutely true.

A few days after my temptation experience, I took my wife and children for a little outing. We drove up from the Valley of the Sun into the beautiful mountains to one of our favorite places, Payson, AZ. It was just fun to see the beauty and enjoy one another. As I drove along one lovely vista, there was a clear voice speaking in my mind, **"If you utter what is true, and not what is false, I will be as thy mouth."** I was humbled and amazed. That was the first time I ever heard God speak to me in an audible voice. I knew it was Him and I reflected soberly. I had long been guilty of exaggerating when I reported things that had happened and I knew this was a warning not to stray from the truth, and a promise that He would speak through me.

I felt strongly that I needed an experienced human pilot. With Jim Johnston's encouragement, I called up Dennis Bennett: *"Your tape launched me; now I need an overall sense of where the Holy Spirit is taking us."* He said, "Come on up and see!" So, Tuesday, January 2, 1963, I flew to Seattle and spent four unforgettable days with Dennis and Elberta and St. Luke's Episcopal Church. A failing little parish (which the Bishop was about to close) had been brought into fullness of life in the Holy Spirit in three years. I was like Alice in Wonderland. I saw all the New Testament gifts and ministries incorporated in a denominational church and the fruit was terrific and attractive. St. Luke's gave me powerful motivation in terms of what could be at Chandler.

Dennis warned me about how the enemy would act to hinder the work of the Holy Spirit, and taught me how to overcome the enemy. He stressed the importance of honesty and openness. His main message was, "Fear not, trust the Lord, trust His Word, and let the Holy Spirit guide you." He, himself, modeled absolute faith. He sent me home with a book, "Ever Increasing Faith" by Smith Wigglesworth. Dennis continued to be my friend and mentor until his death in 1991.

As people found renewal in the Holy Spirit, prayer groups became places where they kindled one another in their desire for God and sharing what was happening to them by His grace. Jim & Virginia Johnston opened their home for a Tuesday evening time of sharing and waiting on the Lord in prayer. That group became a lot like the Swink group I had visited in Phoenix. The Spirit was poured out powerfully there and the meetings enabled people to experience the Presence of the Lord and take their first steps in receiving and learning to use spiritual gifts like tongues, words of knowledge, prophecy and healing. There were unforgettable nights of "Heaven came down and glory filled my soul;" we went forth with "joy unspeakable" to share with others the wonders of God.

There were days of agony to match the glories. I/we made mistakes and hurt people. At least three times we assured individuals they would be healed and told others, too, and shortly afterward they died.[9] In our zeal, we were sometimes rude and came off acting superior. The worst thing is, I was so consumed with doing ministry I neglected my own children and, most of all, my wife.[10] Most evenings I was not at home; I was ministering to others, I was talking too much and not listening enough. Nevertheless, in all my failures, the Lord was incredibly gracious.

We had lots of help. God sent us people who were like angels. Soon after the Spirit fell on me, my friend Gordon called me from Phoenix. "Corrie ten Boom[11] is in town. She's looking for a place to speak Sunday night!" *"Who's she? It's a funny sounding name."* "She

---

[9] i.e., the Murphree child. See Appendix C.

[10] In seminary we were actually taught, by some, that our ministry was to come first. It was common for missionaries to leave their children at home or boarding schools while they devoted themselves to their work.

[11] For more about Corrie ten Boom see Appendix D.

was put in a Nazi concentration camp for sheltering Jews. She came out with a message that Jesus is victor over the horrors of life. She was knighted by the Queen of Holland." I took a leap of faith and set things up for a Sunday night service. Was I ever glad. She was a 72-year old woman radiant with love, joy and peace and she spoke on the second coming of Christ. It was a totally fresh perspective. I can still hear her reading Phillip's translation of the New Testament, "A Bible that even the dumb Dutch can understand." She dared to say, "Pre-Post-A-Millennial ---- Preposterous. We can expect Jesus to come very soon, we don't know which day He will come, but we even do not know one day that He cannot come. Are you, yourself, prepared? Don't allow your faith to be weakened by compromises. Surrender 100% to the Lord, where there is bondage, a sin in your life. Don't harden your heart, but confess and be cleansed." She never tired of saying, "**The earth will be filled with the glory of the Lord as the waters cover the sea."** Habakkuk 2:13

Everyone was impacted. She was a pure channel of grace and salvation. We had to hear more. Fortunately, she was able to come back for a week of meetings in January 1964 and then again in the winter of '66. She taught morning and night. In between, she taught me much and had me with her as she counseled and prayed for others. Several things stood out for me: 1. The wonder of God's forgiving love; "Jesus buries our sins in the depths of the sea and puts out a sign, 'No fishing.'" 2. God gives what He commands; "Jesus, I cannot forgive him (the guard at Ravensbruck), give me Your forgiveness."[12] 3. We are called to be filled

---

[12] "The Hiding Place" by Corrie ten Boom, page 198.

with the Holy Spirit so as to be overcoming witnesses for Jesus. 4. "We are in a war – we must put on the whole armor of God daily (Ephesians 6)". Her greatest message was the most important lesson they learned in the concentration camp – Jesus brings life out of suffering and death. As Betsey said, "There is no pit so deep that He is not deeper still."

Corrie used a memorable object lesson to illustrate this truth. The essence of what she said and did was, "One day the devil struck a blow at Willy. Poor Willy was knocked down. But at the lowest place, Willy cried out to the Lord and the Lord saved him and raised him up to a new life (as she said this, she slammed a ball against the floor and caught it on the rebound). It wasn't long before the devil struck Willy another blow and down he went in great pain and loss. But there, Jesus came to him and said, **"There is no pit so deep that I cannot come to you. Confess your sin and know that I forgive you."** Then Jesus raised him up higher than before (and with that, she bounced the ball and caught it over her head). Then one day the devil whacked Willy harder than ever, so he went down, down into the deepest, darkest pit ever. But 'lo and behold, Jesus was there before him and raised him up to the highest heaven" (as she said this, Corrie would slam the ball so that it shot up and bounced off the ceiling). Then with a look of immense joy on her face, she imitated the devil saying, "Where'd Willy go?"

In the mornings of her first week with us, her teammate Conny took part of the time to teach us about walking in the light, which means being quick to admit our sins and failings to others, to ask forgiveness, and being quick to forgive and be gracious to those who have hurt us. Two mornings Corrie taught on the dangers of the occult and how to pray about past involvement with mediums and psychics. To learn more about this teaching and about Corrie, see Appendix D.

We had a number of remarkable conversions at Chandler.[13] There was Ted, who read the Gospel of Mark in one sitting and then wanted to run up and down his street shouting, "Hear this Good News!" I asked him to join the church – he said, "Not until I can bring two others." He asked God to impress upon him who he should befriend. Then, as he proceeded to befriend two of the toughest prospects in town, he prayed for them and shared with them until they started coming to church with him. Ted also became one of our youth leaders.

There was Howard, the dirty, morose, foul-mouthed mechanic who received Christ as Lord and was delivered from obscenity and depression in one day. He went to the service stations and parts house where he had worked, apologized for his filthy behavior and speech and declared the redemption Jesus wrought. He was a faithful and loving witness all his days.

There was the high school agnostic who wanted to know if he could have the certainty of the Apostles. I challenged him to read the Gospels with the prayer, "If you are the Risen Lord, please reveal yourself to me." He went after that and he also fasted. Then one day he burst in to tell me he awoke that morning to trumpet music. The music built up to an overwhelming crescendo, and he saw beautiful clouds and in the midst, coming toward him, was a pillar of light. It was

---

[13] Most years we took in more people by confession of faith than by letter of transfer.

blinding in brilliance and engulfed him with glory; he was overcome with the fear of God – he fell on his knees weeping and confessing his unworthiness and praying for forgiveness. Before long he felt wonderfully clean and new. As he related this, glory and joy radiated from his face. He went on to lead prayer groups at Grand Canyon College.

Then there was Art. At the request of his wife I went to see him at the trailer court where he was the owner/manager. Culturally he was a Jew and had been the rear gunner in a torpedo bomber in WWII. I found him walking his dog, so I walked with him and engaged in the usual chitchat. All the while I was praying how I might talk to him about Christ. I found out he did not believe in God but he was respectful of those who did. I asked him, *"What is the greatest problem you face in your work?"* He said, "My mother." He then complained she called almost every day and was always butting into his business and his family. He wished she would get lost. So I proposed to him, *"You know there is a God and He cares about you and He can help you with your problem."* I said, *"Here's an idea for you. Why not say, 'God, if you are real, I need help with my mother. If you'll tell me what to do, I'll do it.'"* I made sure he understood me. He looked at me quizzically and indulgently. I wished him well and told him I would drop by again. I kept him in prayer. About two weeks later I went back. He was glad to see me and exclaimed "It worked!" He then told me the next day he was sitting in his living room, the phone rang, his wife came in and said, "It's your mother." He said, "I got up fuming under my breath and then remembered what you told me, so I whispered, 'God, if you're real, help me.' I got an answer! He said, '**Try kindness**.' I picked up the phone and said warmly, 'Hello, mother, how are you today?' There was a long pause. I thought maybe she had fainted." I laughed with him and affirmed him and said, *"God really is alive and He did speak to you and I want to encourage you to hear more of what He has to say."* He responded, "I do want to hear," so I gave him a new contemporary translation of the New Testament and encouraged him to read the Gospel of Mark. Periodically I would check back and we would talk about what he was discovering, and before long he welcomed Jesus into his life as Lord and Savior. He was a joyful and faithful Christian to the end.

We saw many healings by Jesus, but did not see anything like people leaping out of wheelchairs. There was "HW." He was a boy of about ten when I first met him. He had had serious brain surgery for a malignant tumor and they were not able to remove it all. The doctors told his parents, who were well known in the church and community as leaders, the tumor would eventually grow back and he would not live to adulthood. Periodically in church he would have a terrible seizure and vomit and have to be taken home. Jim Johnston and I both felt he could be healed. We had some wonderful prayer times with him and then I felt led to have him come to the church during his school recess (his school was right next to the church). I would talk with him about Jesus and His healing power, then lay hands on his head and pray for him for healing. He enjoyed that. I did this weekly for a year or more. He grew up, handicapped somewhat, but the last I knew[14] he was still alive and well.

---

[14] 2012

A few of our people had visions and prophesied. Three days before Christmas "F" called and said she had a word for me. **"You have feared the sword and I will bring the sword upon you."** (Ezekiel 11:8) At that moment, on the desk before me, my Bible was open to Ezekiel 11! I was amazed, then humbled and troubled. I was asking, *"Does God mean my marriage? My church?"* I had always feared division and controversy --- I wrestled with, **"I came not to bring peace, but a sword."** (Matthew 10:34) There was one other powerful prophecy that confirmed Ezekiel 11:8. More and more it was impressed upon me God was in charge and He would lead and I was to trust and obey regardless of the consequences.

Naturally there were times when I was afraid. When I was really honest with myself I knew deep down inside the pathway of the Holy Spirit, as shown in Acts, naturally would lead to trouble. I didn't want to face it but I knew it would be a stretch for my people to accept radical New Testament Christianity. I began to wonder if I had a right to put my wife and children through the inevitable outbreaks and controversies of Acts. As I pondered this, "F" called again and told me to read Psalm 128. When I read it, I broke down and wept –*"God is too wonderfully good. To think that my wife is to be a fruitful vine and my precious children are to be like olive shoots around my table and that we shall be well and blessed in the time to come."*

A year later in late October as the move of the Holy Spirit was increasing, and as some were voicing their fears about it, I was alone in my study when the Word of the Lord came again. I heard very clearly an audible voice in my mind, **"Guard the truth that has**

been given to you." I checked, and sure enough, in 2 Timothy it says, **"Guard the truth that has been entrusted to you."** I knew this was a confirmation of what I had heard the year before on our trip to Payson. I was grateful for these words. They emboldened me to say what was hard to say, especially since I had always had a fear of man, particularly when they frowned and made faces in response to what I was saying.

Early one evening I went to counsel with "E," a young man who had repeatedly tried to commit suicide. My heart began to fill with compassion for him, but I had to leave to teach a Bible study. As I went, I began to pray with a tremendous burden of love for him. I filled up more and more with love; I felt my heart would burst with tender mercy; the bands of love constrained me, and the inner spring overflowed. I knew everything else must wait, I must pray on in the love of God. I began to drive out into the country; driving hither and thither slowly while I prayed in tongues, and the baptism of love increased and the love flowed out. I did not want to cut this communion short; I thought, *"I've been late before, and they'll understand."* Later I thought, *"I'll go late and just tell them why I am late."* As Divine love poured into me, and then out through intercession for "E," I began to realize the tensions and issues of that days' Presbytery meeting were trivial, that only the love of God mattered and to remain detached from all of the quarrelling of the world. I knew everything had to wait and everything paled in significance before the immensity of God's love. A big problem came to mind, but now I felt carelessness about it; the drivenness to do something and the anxiety no longer mattered. The only thing that mattered was to be filled with love and to minister the same, and whatever was done in love was all right. All was of Grace. (I had just started preaching in Galatians.) How true, I had done nothing to deserve this. At about 8:30 PM the intensity of this baptism had diminished enough to head for my Bible study. When I arrived I was all-atremble inside. I was undone with love; I was almost speechless. Thank God I was able to pour out what God had poured into me.

CHAPTER 5

Taking a Break

After seven years at Chandler our church gave us a prolonged vacation to visit our parents back east in the summer of 1964. I was edgy about this trip, realizing I would be with my children 24/7, within the confines of a small car and motel rooms, and I worried about my irritation level and patience. So I determined before anyone was awake I would get up early every morning and seek a quiet place for prayer and a full tank of the Holy Spirit. We took four children in a two-door '59 Ford with a large trunk. Emily was 8, Laura 6, Philip 4 and Amy was 3. Fortunately there was room for all four in the backseat (those were the days before seatbelts and car seats; they stood up much of the time!). We planned carefully. We would drive to a town with a park and while one of us played with the children the other would prepare a meal, including cooked meals. While driving we did a lot of singing of spiritual and fun songs and played games. At nights we stayed in Holiday Inns that took all the children free.

After driving through the southwest we took the northern route to my parents home near Philadelphia.

We especially enjoyed the beautiful Amish farmland. Then my mother arranged for us to stay in an apartment in Ocean City, NJ. While Marilyn and I relaxed on the beach in the mornings, the children went to a Baptist church Vacation Bible School. Emily came home Wednesday to tell us a lady talked to them about accepting Jesus into their hearts. *"Well, did you accept Jesus into your heart?"* And she said, "No. I told her I wanted to do it with my Daddy." At the time I couldn't talk more because my Unitarian in-laws had dropped in for a visit. It was not until they left late that day that Emily said, "Remember, Daddy, you promised we would talk." So I took her in on my bed and explained to her the way of salvation and prayed for her to receive Jesus and had her pray for herself, asking Jesus into her heart. It was all very matter of fact, without display or emotion, but the next morning when we woke up I could hear a lively discussion going on. Emily was in the back room with her sisters and brother telling them she had accepted Jesus and they should too. Laura agreed they should and indicated they would someday. But Emily said, "We're supposed to do it right now. Laura, you want to go to heaven don't you? Well, you can't go to heaven unless you accept Jesus." Her brother and sisters continued to dodge a decision, so Emily completed the sale by saying, "You don't want the devil to get you, do you? Well, if you don't accept Jesus, the devil will get you." Then she led Laura and Philip into our bedroom to sit on our bed and asked me to lead them in a prayer of acceptance. Up until that point, we were in stitches. It was so comical hearing Emily pouring the heat on her siblings, but it was also wonderful. I can still see them sitting on our bed, all bright eyed and eager. It was precious. Right afterwards, Philip lived up to his name and went after Amy, but she was a little perplexed by it all and started to cry so we came to her rescue. (A few years later she made her decision.) In the following days Emily witnessed to her friends and another teacher at the Bible School. For some time to come Emily would declare to all of our company what had happened. I can tell you, this was all abnormal for Presbyterians. For some reason in Sunday school it didn't occur to us to talk like this to children.

For a couple of weeks the children got to know their grandparents and cousins on both sides of the family. They also visited some of my friends who had children their ages. They jumped in a haymow, picked cherries, rode in a pony cart, swam in many pools and enjoyed themselves. We took in all the sights in Philadelphia and Washington, DC and eventually came home by the southern route. At the end I felt as if I had done pretty well for a hypertensive Dad. For the most part I was able to relax and enjoy my children like I wanted to.

CHAPTER 6

God's Abundance

Within a year of my baptism, the stirrings of the Holy Spirit not only were bringing exciting new life that was attracting new people, but it also caused people to oppose what was happening out of fear our church would change from a traditional one to something too radical. In those days the fear of anything Pentecostal was enormous. Though experiences of tongues and healings mostly happened at the Johnston home and in counseling, rumors spread through the community alarming people. Incredibly, the strongest opposition was against the laying on of hands and healing prayer. In spite of the opposition the church began to grow. It grew from a small congregation of about 100 attendees to over 250 regular attendees in three years. People would say, "I started coming here because I sensed the Presence of the Lord." He was working powerfully in every area of the church's life and lives were being transformed by Christ and filled with the Holy Spirit.

I grew up in the Great Depression. Our mindset was: save your pennies and spend as little as possible. God would help us – just enough to get by. There was no philosophy of abundance. Imagine my surprise when I started to think in 1965, *"Wouldn't it be nice if my children could have a pony."* It was insane. We were just getting by, and I was preaching to my church they should give sacrificially, but the thought kept returning. I wanted my children to have this happiness. Since buying a pony was out of the question I thought, *"Maybe somebody in the farms all around us has an old pony they no longer want. Or maybe somebody could even loan us a pony."* Then the thought came, *"Lord, if this could be Your will, let the little farm for sale up the street be bought by a friend. Then I'd have a place to keep a pony."*

A few weeks later the farm sold to one of my members, Norman! When I saw him, I said, *"Norman, what are you going to do with that farm?"* He said, "I'm going to board horses." The wheels were turning.

I was talking to Butch, one of our youth leaders. I told him of my dream. He said, "I know of a riding school up in Prescott where they need horses all summer but in the winter they are looking for people to board them free down here in the Valley of the Sun." I said, *"Do you suppose ….?"*

He said he'd check. Next thing I knew I was with Butch in his pickup pulling a horse trailer on our way to Prescott. We were so excited he forgot his speed and was pulled over by the Highway Patrol, but we made it to Bud Brown's riding camp. He had a whole corral of horses and ponies. I asked him if he had a pony suitable for my little children. He said, "How many do you want?" He showed me a pair of Welsh ponies. They were trained to ride children and to pull a cart and had been in several Hollywood movies. They were named Nip and Tuck. It was early December. I asked, *"What would it cost me to take both of these until spring?"* (One for my kids and one for Normans'.) He said, "Preacher, it won't cost you nothin." He went on... "You'll need saddles and bridles. I'll loan you some." I was brimming over with praise to the Lord. We loaded up Nip and Tuck in Butch's trailer and started home.

It was late in the evening when we arrived at our house. I can still see the breath from the horses' nostrils in the taillights of the horse trailer. Somehow my children got wind of our arrival and came running out of the house in their Dr. Denton's. They went crazy jumping up and down and squealing with delight that their strict Daddy had arrived with two ponies. It was hard to get them to go to sleep that night. Before long Jean and Norman were teaching them how to ride, along with their children, and we were on our way to two years of unforgettable fun. This was life changing for my concept of God. He not only gives daily bread, but also often gives bread with jam on it.

Grace often comes in bunches. On top of the ponies, my church decided to add a family room, laundry room, bathroom and master bedroom for us. Our men did all the work in a short time and it was so good for our expanding family.

CHAPTER 7

Fear Not

In 1966 my wife wanted us to have another boy but because of our knowledge of genetics we did not believe she would conceive another boy. She began to urge me to consider adoption. She got in touch with a Christian lawyer whose avocation was to help young women with unwanted pregnancies to find a home for their babies. In January 1967 we all drove to the lawyer's house and picked up a week old baby boy and named him Samuel Chase. The kids were all excited and the church was all-agog, and showered us with baby stuff.

However, by spring the opposition at my church complained so much to the Presbytery[15] they appointed an administrative commission to investigate our church and recommend a solution. The five-member commission held meetings with me, our elders, the disaffected people and studied our church and its' records. It felt like five months of inquisition and intimidation and though the Lord gave us strength

---

[15] The overseeing organization of local Presbyterian churches made up of elders and ministers of all the churches in a County or City area.

it was obvious we were up against heavy prejudice. Things came to a head on October 30, 1967 at a special called meeting of Phoenix Presbytery. At that time, the commission sought to show my leadership was divisive because I had introduced speaking in tongues, healing with the laying on of hands and anointing with oil, and exorcism. They claimed such practices were disruptive of the peace and unity of the church, unimportant for an effective ministry and biblically unnecessary. In sum, I had caused much trouble over inconsequential matters.

The committee report took all afternoon, and then it was my turn to talk. The 100 ministers and elders present were already weary. I had a very bad cold and could barely speak. My head was whirling. I felt the total absence of Jesus. I asked that we take a break. While the Presbytery had dinner, I took refuge in the Moderator's office; I asked the Lord to clear my head and give me power to speak.

When I rose before the Presbytery to speak from the pulpit, I was at peace and resolute – I would not argue or fight my cause.[16] As I began to speak words of courtesy and gratitude for the time spent on our case, the warm, strong Presence of the Spirit came over me. I spoke of the resurrected, ascended, glorified Christ who poured out His Spirit so as to lift us up and identify us with him in bringing healing and deliverance and joy to desperate people. I told them He had so overwhelmed me by His Spirit that I had frequently been led to do the same things He and the

---

[16] The chairman had already told me what they would ask of me, and I knew what my answer would be and the Lord had told me for days, **"You're going."**

apostles did. I quoted, **"He who believes in Me will also do the works I do; and greater works than these will he do because I go to the Father."** *(John 14:12)* I told them about JM. He was full of hate and condemnation and so sick with bronchitis and asthma he had to sit up in a recliner to sleep. Having discerned a demon in him, two of us prayed deliverance prayer for him in tongues and also lay on hands for healing in my office. He was marvelously delivered, healed and filled with the Holy Spirit and became a man of joy and love. He was well known in town and he went around asking forgiveness of the people and his family who had endured his misery and abuse.

I did not speak long; then there was a questioning of my views and me. The Lord stood by me; my mind was clear and calm. I was able to answer carefully and with humility for my mistakes and convictions.

Finally the recommendations of the commission were voted through and the Moderator had me stand and faced me solemnly while he intoned: "Will you, Rev. Robert C. Whitaker, in obedience to your ordination vows ... promising subjection to your brethren in the Lord, promise to cease and desist as follows with regard to the 'gifts of the Spirit' at issue. Neither support, counsel, lead, interpret, teach, or participate with anyone else anywhere in speaking in tongues, exorcism of evil spirits, and healing by the formal laying on of hands or anointing with oil as long you are a member of the Presbytery of Phoenix?"

I answered, "My conscience is captive to the Word of God; I cannot cease and desist what Christ has called me to do in faith and love." Then I read from the Presbyterian Constitution (G1.0307), "The Holy

Scriptures are the only rule of faith and manners; that no church governing body ought to pretend to make laws to bind the conscience of their own authority; and that all their decisions should be founded upon the revealed will of God." And then I said, "God help me, here I stand." [17]

When I came down from the platform, I came down a free man with my integrity intact; the peace and love of God flooded my heart; I knew already what my punishment would be, but I knew He would wonderfully see me and mine through it. So the Presbytery proceeded to expel me from the ministry of the Chandler church and decreed my family and I would have to be out of the manse in three months and the church would be taken over by another and the elders loyal to my views would also be put out of office. Though it was a blow, I never felt it. It was as if I was shielded in a circle of blessing. Great love overcame my heart; I could feel no hurt. I was flooded with the love of Christ and love for the two-thirds of the Presbytery who voted against me. I told the elder who represented my opponents I loved her without any reservation.

For at least two weeks after my sentence I felt I was walking with the King. It seemed He had put a robe around me, had caused me to walk more erectly than ever before and was saying to me, "**I'm proud of you and I'm with you.**" It was glorious. I had wonderful peace and so did my wife. We were assured the Lord would take care of us. During the next months as I sought for a new place of service we were showered with affirmations, love and gifts. We were able to pay off all our debts and buy things we needed. Many of my

---

[17] I purposely used the famous words of Luther.

people wanted me to form a new independent church in defiance of the Presbytery, but I knew in my heart I couldn't do that. The Lord wanted me to take my witness to the denomination, so I tried to find another Presbyterian church. It was fruitless. All they had to do was call Phoenix and they would come back to me and say, "We're sorry, Mr. Whitaker, we have nothing for you."

After a few months Murray Russell, Associate Pastor, Glendale Presbyterian Church California, called. He said, "We want you over here at Glendale." I said, "*You must not know much about me.*" He said, "We know all about you and we want you," to which I replied, "*How much do you know about me?*" "We talked to your friend George Carpenter." Then I knew they did know. Twice they had me over to Glendale to sell me on coming there. Murray needed help; they had no Sr. Pastor and needed another Associate. I turned them down twice. It was a big, scary, conservative bastion. Murray got on the phone. He said, "You haven't prayed enough. You think you're not supposed to come but for your own good I'm telling you in God's Name you're supposed to come and I'm going to make it easy. We'll fly you over here five days a week then we'll fly you back home to Arizona to be with your family. We'll pay you well. You stay for a month. If you don't like it, you can leave after a month. You don't have anything to do and nobody else wants you, you've got nothing to lose." I knew I had to give it a try. At that time 400 Presbyterian ministers were trying to get into Southern California but there were no vacancies. I didn't want to go, and the door was wide open!

Meanwhile, my Presbyterian minister friend Brick Bradford (a former lawyer) was urging me to appeal to the General Assembly of the United Presbyterian Church what the Presbytery of Phoenix had done to me.[18] My mentor, Dr. John Mackay[19] concurred with this. I was hesitant because during the winter I had appealed to the Synod[20] of Arizona and they had reinforced the decision of Phoenix Presbytery against me. It was a demoralizing experience. But Brick said if I would appeal he would leave his home in Oklahoma and come to Glendale and do much of the work to put together a legal appeal to the General Assembly. I knew I had to do it. I had previously met with Dr. Mackay and twenty other Charismatic Presbyterian ministers. We had all agreed if any of us got in trouble for our witness, we would appeal it to the General Assembly. Perhaps we could strike a blow for freedom for the Holy Spirit in the denominational churches.

I was at Glendale five days a week all during March and April, during which time Brick came and we formulated my appeal to General Assembly. Then, through Murray, I told the Session[21] I was going to make my appeal to General Assembly and I did not think they would vindicate me so I would then resign and leave the Presbyterian Church. A Session representative met with me and told me win or lose they wanted me back. I was deeply moved. Nevertheless, to be safe, I cleaned

---

[18] The General Assembly is made up of elder and minister representatives from all the Presbyteries in the country.

[19] For more about Dr. Mackay see Appendix E.

[20] A Synod is usually a statewide organization, which has authority over the Presbyteries in that State.

[21] A Session is the governing body of a local Presbyterian church made up of the preaching ministers and elders.

out my desk and set my face to go to Minneapolis, MN for the opening meeting with the Permanent Judicial Commission of the General Assembly of the United Presbyterian Church.

CHAPTER 8

Here Come the Judges

Monday night, May 13, I met Brick in Minneapolis. It was great to see him but I was in a mood of pessimism. I knew no matter what happened God would use it for His glory, but I tended to believe I would lose my case and that was okay because then I would feel free to withdraw from the Presbyterian Church and go independent. That was very attractive because I was weary with bucking the Presbyterian establishment and rather dreaded the responsibility that would inevitably come with winning. In February I had moved my family to a little rented farmhouse[22] east of Chandler and I wanted to settle down there. By May many of my people from the Presbyterian Church had formed an independent church and they were pleading

---

[22] I loved that little acre. It had an orchard, a pony and a large chicken house full of chickens and ducks – it was something I had wanted since I was a little boy. We added rabbits and a calf and the children loved to feed the calf his bottle and ride the pony. I wanted to live there forever and forget the world. Unfortunately, Marilyn didn't like the place because there were so many spiders.

with me to be their pastor and build together our vision of a Spirit-filled church.

Brick and I stayed outside of Minneapolis at Bethany. I loved it there. Bethany was a community of Spirit-filled missionaries and trainees and their families. They were mostly Swedes and Norwegians. They were wonderful to us. They housed us and fed us free of charge and provided a car every day for us to go in and out to Minneapolis. The atmosphere of peace and harmony and industry was contagious. The meetings for prayer and worship were vitalizing.

Our hearing before the Permanent Judicial Commission was Tuesday night, May 14th, in the Land-O-Lakes room of the Leamington Hotel. It was a small room with a U-shaped table for the fourteen judges[23] to sit around and a short table at one end of the room with chairs bunched behind it for the complainant (me) and the respondents[24] (the brass from Phoenix and Arizona).

I opened the hearing with a forty-minute testimony; I had settled in my mind as a result of meditating on Acts and counsel from my father, I should give my testimony. My father had said my Brief and Complaint[25] covered the technical details and the substantive argument, but I should give the judges a desire to vindicate me by

---

[23] Seven of the fourteen were distinguished older Presbyterian ministers. The other seven were professional lawyers and judges from secular courts.

[24] Phoenix Presbytery and the Synod of Arizona had sent their top men, Dr. Charles Ehrhardt, Moderator, Commission Chairman Rev. Goodenberger, Rev. Dale Hewitt, Moderator of the Synod of Arizona, and an elder from the Commission. Dr. David Sholin, probably the best preacher in the Synod, failed to show up.

[25] For copies of the Brief and Complaint, see the author. Dr. John Mackay said they were "luminous and potent."

simply telling my story.[26] Before I gave my testimony I read the oath, or vow, which the commission wanted me to take and said, *"There was a time when I could easily have assented to that promise because I was the product of a liberal education and did not fully believe in the Bible. But now I want to explain to you why I could not take it."* Then I told about my experience of the Risen Lord and the bestowal of the Spirit and His gifts and how it was consistent with the constitutional rule of scripture. I specifically pointed out Jesus had called me to heal as much as to preach, and despite potential division I must obey Him. I read the passage where Jesus tells His disciples not to forbid the casting out of demons. I went on to say the Presbytery should have studied, investigated and regulated the gifts instead of banning them. Further, they had placed me in an impossible position – Jesus commanded me to heal, they asked me to promise not to do so in the way He and His apostles did; Jesus commanded me to cast out demons, they wanted me to promise not to do so; Jesus gave me the blessing of tongues, they asked me to be silent about it.

Dale Hewitt spoke; then Dr. Ehrhardt spoke devastatingly and convincingly. He portrayed me as a divisive and misguided troublemaker earnestly contending for things unimportant. He was very persuasive that something had to be done to save the church from me and they had done the best thing.

---

[26] I had always wondered why Paul's testimony is included three times in the Book of Acts. Then one day my eyes were opened. This was God's way of impressing the early Christians what they should do when they were called up before authorities.

When they were done, Brick closed with a few answering arguments. I wanted him to tear apart my opponents with incisive logic. Fortunately he chose not to do that. Instead he sought to prove the vows the Presbytery wanted me to take were illegal.

Then came the questions from the judges. I was amazed they were very kind to me, but they really went after the respondents. The first question by a judge from St. Louis (as he leaned across the desk and looked at my accusers) was, "Will you please show me anywhere in scripture or the Constitution of the Presbyterian Church anything that would justify what you did to this man?" My opponents were sputtering.[27] I believed then I was getting a fair trial and, whatever the outcome, I would be most respectful of the expert and fair manner in which they went about their business.[28]

I had to wait one week for the judgment to be announced. During that week I attended the meetings of the General Assembly. For me it was a time of sharing with old teachers and colleagues and friends. As for the legislative meetings, I felt there was much steam, many wheels turning, and much energy in the flesh and little of real impact happening. Nevertheless, I am grateful for a democratic church where many people have a chance to influence the decisions that are made for the wellbeing and mission of the church.

---

[27] Later on another judge asked of them, "What was your objection: division, or the kind of preaching being done? You objected to what he taught and so you decided for the minority. In effect a judgmental decision – isn't that what you're saying? Were you saying, 'We are not going to allow this kind of ministry to occur in a Presbyterian Church?'"

[28] For the story behind the story see Appendix E.

Tuesday, May 21, 1968 was a beautiful day. There had been a fair amount of rain and some chilly weather the past week but this day was perfect. You must understand my state of mind. I was still pessimistic. Every day I had driven in to General Assembly in Minneapolis and at night I would drive back to Bethany. I quickly saw the parallel. During the last week of His life, Jesus spent every evening with Mary and Martha in Bethany; every day He went into the big city of Jerusalem and the week would end with His crucifixion. Monday I was more depressed than usual. I had told my friend and mentor John Strock why I wouldn't mind losing. Tuesday night he sat with me in the balcony of the great hall where the 800 commissioners were gathered to hear the preliminary judgments of the Permanent Judicial Commission. All the doors were shut and the fourteen judges came out on the raised stage dressed in black robes and the assembly was called to order as a Court of the Presbyterian Church. For two hours we heard details of judicial cases the judges had decided before mine. When they began to report on my case, it sounded ominous. The presiding judge outlined the story of my case from the Presbytery point of view. I leaned over and whispered to the Strocks. I could tell from the tone they were laying the foundation for denying my appeal. But after showing the Presbytery had cause to act in my case they declared the nub of the problem was the oath they had asked me to take. Then they read the oath out loud. It seemed the whole assembly gasped together when they heard it. The presiding judge then said they would not rule on the biblical and theological issues because the Assembly had already appointed a special committee to study them and report back.[29] They then stated unanimously no judicatory has the right to require any minister or elder to take any vow in addition to their ordination and installation vows. Therefore, they said, the oath was unconstitutional and my complaint was sustained.[30] The Assembly then voted on the judges' decision and, with only one dissenting vote, confirmed it. They then directed the Presbytery and Synod to delete the oath from their practice, and since I did not want reinstatement, they should apologize to me.

I was floored. I was more deeply moved than ever before and was broken up inside and fighting back the tears. I was unprepared to win. It was very overwhelming, very humbling. What meant more to me was I had won in spite of the fact I represented a very unpopular, despised minority point of view, and that few believed I could buck the establishment and win.[31] As I called Marilyn, Murray Russell and my father I cried unashamedly with pure relief and amazement.

The newspapers got hold of the story and did it justice. The Minneapolis Star Tribune said, "A minister

---

[29] As a result of my controversy with the Phoenix Presbytery, and at my request, the Phoenix Presbytery had twice overtured the General Assembly to study and recommend what the Church's stance should be in regard to the freedom of the Presbyterian ministry and the gifts of the Holy Spirit at issue. Two other Presbyteries had asked for the same thing and the Stated Clerk had urged the Assembly to do so.

[30] The main thing that caused the judges to sustain my complaint was the matter of the vow and that was the one thing that Brick had most persuasively argued.

[31] Before I had made my appeal, our Synod executive had warned me that I could never win and it would be ruinous to my career as a Presbyterian minister.

who refused to promise he would not engage in 'speaking in tongues,' exorcising evil spirits and faith healing has been upheld by the United Presbyterian Church's General Assembly here. The Assembly, sitting as the highest court of the denomination, ruled the Presbytery of Phoenix, AZ did not have the authority to exact such a promise from the Rev. Robert C. Whitaker, Chandler, AZ." The Phoenix Republic also covered it well, and the Los Angeles Times had a four-column article.

Vincent Synan, the Pentecostal historian[32] said, "It was a great moral victory for all charismatics in the mainline churches. But the victory did not end with the successful appeal. As a result of the Whitaker case, every Presbyterian minister was protected from arbitrary removal from his or her parish by a Presbytery on grounds of involvement in the Charismatic Renewal."

---

[32] "The Century of the Holy Spirit" page 171

CHAPTER 9

Under Pharaoh

My first week at Glendale began with a jolt: I was in Chandler; Murray called from California early Saturday morning March 2nd; he was sick; I would have to preach Youth Sunday "tomorrow." *"Lord, what's a good biblical youth theme?"* Joseph came to mind. I read his story and it got all over me! I, too, had been unwise about my dreams; my brothers had turned on me, roughed me up and expelled me. Despite the General Assembly partial victory, I was on my way to servitude in Egypt; I would be in confinement for a while, but eventually I would be free to help my brothers find bread. What they did was ultimately for my good. God would use it to save and bless many lives. I was to fully forgive and go down to Egypt (Glendale) and serve humbly.

Despite the Joseph paradigm, in the spring of '68 I seesawed back and forth. I longed to stay with my spiritual friends in Chandler while my conscience, relatives, and solid colleagues urged me to go on with

Glendale.[33] Letting go was wrenching, but nevertheless in late June my family moved to Glendale. July 1st we bought a house by faith ($30,000!).

We were warmly welcomed at Glendale Presbyterian Church, but dear Murray had to step down to return to his mission in Africa. I missed him terribly and I found the new interim minister difficult to work for, but I pressed on with the ministry of teaching and pastoral care.

Late in the year the new senior minister arrived and took over. I could readily think of him as Pharaoh. He was a huge man. He was very dominant, very bright and was able to quickly size up the situation, organize the ministry and program of the church in a comprehensive and effective way. He was a powerful preacher, but I missed the warmth and intimacy of the Holy Spirit. I was being urged to implement a program that was not my style and increasingly it became clear in our discussions he was not hospitable to my point of view. I began to wonder if I had made a terrible mistake. Meanwhile, my friends in Chandler renewed their pleas that I come back and be the pastor of the new Trinity Community Church.[34]

By early spring of 1969 I was tormented with, *"Shall I stay or go back?"* At one point I told Trinity Church I would come back, and Pharaoh that I would be leaving.

---

[33] Some people said, "The good shepherd lays down his life for the sheep, but the hireling leaves them when he sees the wolf coming." (John 10:11-12, RCW version) This text tore at me. How could I leave my scattering sheep in Chandler?

[34] Also, the General Assembly's Committee on the Work of the Holy Spirit had postponed their expected report until 1970. I had hoped they would substantially support my teaching on the power and gifts of the Holy Spirit.

We made arrangements to sell our house and had a buyer lined up. The inner debate became hellish. I had no peace. My mind was racing like a squirrel in a cage. Emotionally I was up and down and could not concentrate. My wife pleaded with me to settle it one way or the other. I feared I was having a nervous breakdown. Finally I leveled with Pharaoh and told him the whole story including the Joseph analogy. He called together seven of the Glendale pillars. They prayed it out with me. I called Trinity and backed out of my commitment. They were very gracious. I knew responsibility and faithfulness would have to take precedence over feelings.

In 1970 the Special Committee on the Work of the Holy Spirit presented their final report and it was adopted by the General Assembly of the United Presbyterian Church. It was a groundbreaking document that put the Presbyterian Church officially on record as the first non-Pentecostal denomination favorable to the gifts of the Holy Spirit. Before, the major Protestant denominations considered the supernatural gifts as having ceased with the death of the apostles. The report proved from the most recent psychological studies that people who spoke in tongues were psychologically healthy as a whole[35] and the gift was not to be despised, but to be accepted when practiced according to 1 Corinthians 14 (however, it said tongues should not be emphasized). The report was also favorable to the healing ministry with the laying on of hands and anointing with oil. The report stated ministers, presbyteries and church members should be tolerant of the charismata as long as they are practiced decently and in order. The

---

[35] Most people in America believed that tongue speakers were nuts.

section on exorcism was very conservative, speaking of "grave dangers" in exorcism, but it did not forbid such deliverance ministries. The report had some wonderful passages such as, "The outpouring of the Spirit bestows upon Christians gifts and lights and powers. Where these are lacking, there is reason to ask whether in pride or sloth the community .... has perhaps evaded this endowment, thus falsifying its' relationship to its' Lord."[36] The bottom line was the Committee and the Assembly substantially upheld what I had practiced and taught! This report became the model for many similar reports done at later dates by other denominations throughout the world. It meant a new day in the relationship between Protestant Christians and the growing Pentecostal-Charismatic movement. Since the formation of the Committee and its' work grew out of my case, it opened doors for me to be invited to speak of the work of the Holy Spirit worldwide. To God be the Glory!

At Glendale Presbyterian Church I was the Minister of Community and World Mission. I also did much of the pastoral calling, teaching and handled most of the funerals. My biggest responsibility was to train people in evangelistic calling and to organize and lead our calling on visitors and to help people accept Christ as their Lord and Savior and be trained as members of His church. So I had plenty to do and good things were happening, but I was getting more and more depressed. Even my children commented, "Daddy you don't preach like you used to." I believed I was depressed because of the way Pharaoh was treating me. To me, he was demanding, critical and inconsiderate.

[36] Dr. Karl Barth.

He was so knowledgeable that he could have won any quiz program in any category. Next to him and his photographic memory, I felt dumb.

Fortunately, one of my best friends, Newton Maloney, was a Clinical Psychologist and he was teaching at Fuller Seminary. In late 1969, I had enrolled at Fuller to work on a doctorate[37], so it was convenient to see Newton. I told him what Pharaoh was doing to me. Right away he asked, "Have you told him how you feel?" and I said, *"No."* He asked, "Why not?" *"He does not have any time for me outside of official staff meetings and church business."* Then he said, "Come on, Bob, you're his right hand man; of course he has time for you." *"He is so scheduled it would be weeks before he could talk with me."* "Bob, why can't you insist on time to talk out your issue?" *"Do you want to know the truth? I'm afraid of him. He is so intimidating anything I would say, he would reduce me to a pile of ashes."* "So what are you going to do Bob?" *"I think I'm going to quit."* "And go away defeated?" I knew I couldn't do that. So I went back to Pharaoh. I caught him in the hallway and said, *"I need to talk."* Immediately he replied, "What about?" *"About us."* "What about us?" *"Look, I'm hurting, I've got to talk."* He said, "I'm too busy, my calendar is full, but I'll give you my day off. You come to my apartment October 8th in the morning. It better be important." I wanted to be sure I didn't waste his time so I made notes on seven 3x5 cards of all the times he put me down and made life difficult for me.

---

[37] I did not finish my doctoral work. I felt it was more important to be at home with my family. My doctoral mentor was Dr. George Ladd. He liked my work. I was out to prove the charismata never had disappeared from Christian history.

Nine o'clock sharp I arrived at his apartment. He sat behind a desk; I sat opposite him on a lower chair. I was all prayed up and all choked up. This was scary. I could hardly speak. The words came as if I was spitting up sawdust. I was so unaccustomed to speak boldly to people who intimidated me. I started by saying, *"I've been hurting a long time. I should have kept short accounts. Please understand, everything I have against you I'm guilty of myself, but I've got to tell you how I feel."* Then I went down the list of all the things he had said and done which were hurtful. He listened very carefully. It took a long time. Then he said, "Well, you did have a lot to say and I will answer you, but first I want to commend you. Today, at last, I met the real Bob Whitaker. I knew behind all the smiles, something was wrong." Then he leaned his massive body across the desk toward me and boomed, "Why didn't you ever tell me these things before?" *"I was afraid."* Then he asked, "What were you afraid of? *"I was afraid you would blow me out of the water."* Then one by one he went over my list in order. For some things he confessed he was guilty as charged and asked my forgiveness. Other things he gave me explanations that helped me to see I was partly right and partly wrong and I thanked him for the correction. And in a few things he felt I had him wrong and he defended himself admirably. I asked his forgiveness. Almost three hours had gone by. He said, "This has been very good. We must do this more often and speak the truth to one another." I agreed. I felt wonderfully relieved. I had been heard and I had been given grace to receive peacefully the response I so much feared. Then I hurried away because I was already late for an appointment.[38]

This meeting was one of the most formative events of my entire life. I had spoken the truth in love to one who I later described as a lion. I had put my head in his mouth and behold there were no teeth. I went away exhilarated, liberated from the depression that had gripped me. I was in awe of the power of truth and I knew it was the Holy Spirit.[39]

In late 1970 Pharaoh gave me what I wanted. I put together a proposal asking the Session to appoint a committee of our medical professionals and people of prayer to investigate the Christian healing ministry in the Los Angeles area and to make suggestions concerning our own healing services at GPC.[40] I was named Staff Advisor to the committee. The Chairman was Dr. Donald Polhemus.[41] It was an endless adventure to see our professional medical people make visits to healing services and interview healers and people who had received healing ministry and gradually discover Christ was still healing. The conclusion of their studies was interviewing Dr. Jay Rayzooli, a distinguished doctor in San Pedro. Tests and xrays had shown a cancerous tumor the size of a fist in his right lung and surgery was scheduled to remove it. He received prayer from his church and then asked that additional xrays

---

[38] I was on my way to meet with Chuck Smith, pastor/founder of Calvary Chapel, who wanted to talk to me about becoming his assistant. I had been planning to say yes, but after the truth encounter I declined his offer.

[39] See my blog, "www.bobsgodblog.blogspot.com, *What if the Hurter Continues to Hurt?*"

[40] Glendale Presbyterian Church.

[41] A member of Mensa Society.

be taken prior to surgery. Much to the amazement of the radiologist, the tumor was completely gone and surgery was cancelled. His health improved rapidly and subsequent tests proved his chest was clear.[42] Having looked at all of the tests and xrays and heard the testimony, Dr. Polhemus said, "It would be a severe strain on credulity to posit any other explanation than to say it was a miracle." The result was that in the fall of 1971 GPC instituted very quiet and orderly Sunday evening services of Communion and prayer for healing with the laying on of hands. All of our staff ministers were involved and Pharaoh discovered to his amazement people even got healed through his prayers.

---

[42] Dr. Rayzooli's four-page testimony is available upon request from the author.

CHAPTER 10

In the Place of Infamy

All during the '60s the visitation of Jesus we experienced at Chandler was happening at various places throughout the United States and the world. By the time I went to Glendale I was in touch with some fifty Presbyterian ministers who had been baptized in the Holy Spirit. In the late '60s, what to our amazement should happen, but increasing numbers of Catholics were experiencing the new birth and overflow of the Holy Spirit. In California Ray Bringham pioneered international renewal meetings, which included classical Pentecostals, denominational charismatics (like myself) and Catholics. For the first time in history Catholics and Protestants together were enjoying meetings where the Holy Spirit was invading with power and joy.

Bringham was invited to bring his group[43] to a conference of the International Ecumenical Fellowship[44] meeting in Salamanca, Spain, August

---

[43] The Interchurch Renewal Ministry
[44] This group (IEF) consisted of European Protestant, Orthodox and Catholic leaders.

1970. They wanted the charismatics to enrich their study of the Holy Spirit! For those days, this was really bold. Ray asked me to go, together with forty-four others. I was excited; this was my first overseas trip. Interested friends chipped in $850 for the round trip.[45] We flew from Los Angeles to Amsterdam and by train and bus reached Salamanca. This is a charming old ecclesiastical and intellectual center where seventy Catholic religious orders resided, and where there are awesome old churches, narrow cobblestone streets and the mystical old Pontifical University. This was once the dread headquarters of the Catholic Inquisition and a place made infamous for stifling any dissent from medieval Catholicism.

The IEF was eagerly awaiting our arrival. They anticipated we would be sectarian, relatively uneducated and Protestant. They were astounded to find we were open minded, well educated and at least half of us were Catholic charismatics. Every day we heard lectures from the best representatives of the various theological perspectives. Also we took turns attending worship services of the respective groups, and discussed with one another our experiences of these new types of worship. We gained new perspective and appreciation. At night after supper (9:30 PM), many of the conference participants flocked to our charismatic prayer meetings held in the collegio and enthusiastically invited us into their homes to hear our testimonies.

---

[45] Most of our group experienced a miraculous provision for the trip.

I will never forget Thursday morning. It was our turn[46] to lead a public service of charismatic worship in a huge cathedral-like church called La Purisima. It was a challenge. So many different people coming from so many different church backgrounds, most of them used to set forms of prayer and elaborate liturgies. They all wondered what would happen. (So did we.) I was called upon to lead out in prayer. It was expected there would then be free and spontaneous prayer and prophecy throughout the sanctuary. As I began to pray, I felt prompted to pray in tongues and then to sing in tongues. I let it rip. The Holy Spirit opened up the whole place and there was a free flowing participation in accordance with 1 Corinthians 14.[47] Jesus was exalted.

After the service our hosts led us to the rear of the dais, which was normally off limits. What should I see there but on either side were iron bars and behind the bars were women dressed in full Catholic habits covering everything but their faces. I asked my host, *"Who are these women?"* He explained they were cloistered nuns who spend their lives in prayer and are not even seen in the sanctuary but were allowed to participate in the service behind the curtain. I could not get over the joyous and child-like expressions on their faces as they warmly welcomed us and expressed their thanksgiving and love for the service of prayer. They were radiant. I was shocked; I had been raised with the propaganda that nuns were unmarriageable

---

[46] David duPlessis, Ray Bringham, Robert Frost, Leland Davis and myself.

[47] This reminded me of the Jim Swink meeting on a grand scale.

old maids who were the Pope's slaves. Their beauty captivated me.

It was ironic to me that in the infamous old places of accusation, torture and excommunication, the love of God and the fellowship of the Holy Spirit was delightful and embracing. Many went away brim full with the Holy Spirit.

Then came a surprise. David duPlessis invited me to join with five other of our leaders to go to Rome to meet with the Vatican Secretariat For the Promotion of Christian Unity.[48] What was I to do? I'd already been gone from home ten days. My children needed me, but God gave me a green light. So off we went on another adventure. As we left sunny Spain and flew over the blue-green Mediterranean Sea, I thought to myself, *"What would Chickie Burns say?"* (He was the snotty Catholic boy who persecuted me when I was little.)

Upon landing in Rome we were taken immediately to the apartment of Cardinal Laronna. He was a Priest from Spain and he greeted us like long-lost Christian brothers. At the time, he was the Pope's right-hand man and had arranged for our meetings with the Secretariat on Unity. He showed us around his lovely apartment overlooking St. Peter's, prayed with us in his little chapel, and let me take a picture of his wonderful portrait of St. Teresa of Avila. The Vatican representatives fed us the most wonderful Italian food I've ever eaten and met with us for three days. The purpose was to discover whether or not there was a basis for ongoing discussions and relationships with

---

[48] This was a pre-arranged meeting. At the last minute one of the team had to drop out due to illness and David invited me to take his place.

the Pentecostal-Charismatic movement. The plan was simple. One by one we shared our faith and experience with the three Catholic Priests appointed to meet with us, and they in turn shared their faith with us. Then we summarized what we had in common, especially our understanding and experience of the Holy Spirit. We also prayed together and there were times when we wept together. Before we adjourned, Cardinal Laronna invited us to go with him and fellowship with him for several days as he vacationed at the Pope's summer residence in the mountains. I desperately wanted to go. I had found a true spiritual brotherhood at the Vatican and I wanted to pursue it further, but my wife and children were tugging at my heart so I headed for home. On the way I meditated on the fact that the Spirit is moving all over the world to bring Christians to discover one another and love one another as Jesus prayed in John 17:21-22, **"That they may all be one; even as thou, Father, art in me, and I in thee, that they also may be in us, so that the world may believe that thou hast sent me. The glory which thou hast given me I have given them, that they may be one even as we are one."** [49]

---

[49] See Appendix F for the outcome of our meeting.

CHAPTER 11

He is Risen Indeed

At GPC funerals were part of my job. I averaged about two a month and many of the burials were at one of the most beautiful cemeteries in the world, Forest Lawn (both Glendale and Hollywood Hills).[50] I considered it a joy and an opportunity to conduct a funeral. It was a chance to help people really believe in the resurrection of Jesus Christ. Most of my professors at Yale would have raised their eyebrows at that comment. They did not believe in the literal bodily resurrection of Jesus. They believed that His Spirit had survived death and the resurrection reports were either exaggerated or myths. After the Holy Spirit fell on me at Chandler, the presence of the Risen Christ was very real to me. I became firmly convinced that He rose in a transfigured body and, as 1 Corinthians 15 points out, His resurrection was the pattern for what will happen to us in the future.

---

[50] I loved the chapels. Architecturally they were charming, conducive to worship and comfortable; Little Church of the Flowers was my favorite. They had one or two canary birds chirping away during the service!

I tried to make it clear to the mourners that the story of Jesus' resurrection is thoroughly grounded in historic fact; it is attested not only by honest Christian historians, but by pagan writers as well. Most importantly, the resurrection of Jesus is one of the most confirmed facts of history.[51] There were hundreds of witnesses who saw him during a period of forty days. Among them were apostles of unimpeachable veracity, who finally confirmed their testimony in triumphant martyr deaths. Josephus, the famous Jewish historian, writing around 100 AD, acknowledged the resurrection.

I felt it most helpful to show that all of nature is a parable of God's resurrection plan for all who believe in Him. One of the poems I quoted often was "Seeds" by John Oxenham: "We drop a seed into the ground, a tiny shapeless thing, shriveled and dry, and in the fullness of its time, is seen a form of peerless beauty, robed and crowned beyond the pride of any earthly queen, instinct with loveliness, and sweet and rare, the perfect emblem of its Maker's care. This from a shriveled seed? – Then may man hope indeed! For man is but the seed of what he shall be ... We know not what we shall be – only this – that we shall be made like Him – as He is." As a gardener I love to point people to gorgeous flowers and then say to them, *"Just think, this beautiful thing grew out of mud. If lilies can grow out of mud, why can't we?"*

---

[51] Dr. Simon Greenleaf, famous professor of law at Harvard, and an expert on how to tell if a witness is lying, wrote a volume on the legal value of the apostolic testimony. He concluded that the resurrection of Christ was one of the best-attested events in history according to the laws of evidence administered in courts of justice. (Pg. 97, "More than a Carpenter" by Josh MacDowell.)

My favorite story was one that was told by Cecil B. DeMille, the famous Hollywood director of dramatic Biblical stories. "One day as I was lying in a canoe a big black beetle came out of the water and climbed into the canoe. I watched it idly for some time. Under the heat of the sun, the beetle proceeded to die. Then a strange thing happened. His glistening black shell cracked all the way down his back. Out of it came a shapeless mass, quickly transformed into brilliantly colored life. As I watched in fascination, there gradually unfolded iridescent wings from which the sunlight flashed a thousand colors. The wings spread wide, as if in worship of the sun. The blue-green body took shape. Before my eyes had occurred a metamorphosis – the transformation of a hideous beetle into a gorgeous dragonfly, which started dipping and soaring over the water. But the body it had left behind still clung to my canoe. I had witnessed what seemed to me a miracle. Out of the mud had come a beautiful new life. And the thought came to me, that if the creator works such wonders with the lowliest of creatures, what may not be in store for the human spirit?"[52]

I must have told that story in the '70s and since several hundred times. Many were touched by it. It helped them to believe the reasonableness of the resurrection of Jesus Christ and of our own resurrection yet to come. I was always fond of pointing out the verse from 1 Corinthians 15:49, **"Just as we have borne the image of the man of dust (Adam), we shall also bear the image of the man of heaven."** And Philippians 3:20-21, **"But our commonwealth is in heaven, and from it we await a savior, the Lord**

---

[52] "The Complete Funeral Manual" by James L. Christenson, pg. 44

Jesus Christ, who will change our lowly body to be like His glorious body, by the power which enables Him even to subject all things to Himself."

Since the New Testament days there have been countless cases of individuals who have had an encounter with the Risen Christ. Many of them have come through dreams and visions, but others have happened in broad daylight in such a way that the persons were convinced it was the Risen Lord as surely as the Apostle Paul's encounter on the Damascus road. The proof of their substantial reality was that the individuals involved were markedly changed, morally and behavior wise. I have had the privilege of knowing such people and being able to interview them. One of them is one of my best friends.

I must say this conviction about the Risen Christ has been highly motivating. When I have preached about it, and above all at funerals, I have given some sort of invitation for people to respond in faith. Usually I say something like, *"If you would like to know more about the resurrected Christ and how you can know Him better, I will be happy to speak to you after the service, or if you wish we can make an appointment to get together later."*

CHAPTER 12

Facing the Truth

One day at home I was yelling at my children. I wish this were the only time. I also at times yelled at my wife. In the midst of my outburst I heard the still, small voice, **"Listen to yourself."** I stopped in midsentence and exclaimed, *"Oh my God, it's my mother all over again."* I was stunned. My older sisters had always said, "Bobby, you're an angry person" and I had denied it. Over the years there were times when I faced it for a while, but now I saw clearly I was angry just like my mother. We had a long history. She had been a very loving mother in my earliest years, but she was also quite fearful and as a result terrifically overprotective and restrictive. In addition, in my teenage years, she was out of control and verbally and physically abusive. Fortunately, that was punctuated with loving and generous behavior.

After my conversion I had tried hard to love her and avoid getting into angry exchanges with her but inevitably we would get into it and I would over react in hurtful responses. I was ashamed of this. I figured the best way to handle her neurotic and abusive behavior was to get away from her. That's what college meant to me, getting away from mother and enjoying the freedom of doing what I wanted to do instead of endless restrictions and scolding. I could have a messy room and go to all the movies I wanted. Once I graduated from seminary I determined I would live far away from Philadelphia. We have seen my first church was in Tennessee, the second in Arizona and the third in California, but I haven't made it to Hawaii yet! Had you asked me whether or not I loved my mother I would have said, *"Of course I do, what do you take me for? I'm a good Presbyterian minister."*

When I did go home to visit, which was seldom, and when my parents came to see us (also seldom), my mother was always welcoming and embracing and thrilled to see me. I would stand there and endure her hugs and kisses and be unable to respond in any loving way. Toward her I had a heart of stone. I could pretend to be loving but I was locked into the same behavior I hated in her. I began to face I couldn't love her because I had never forgiven her. I began to pray, *"Dear Father in Heaven, help me to forgive my mother and to love her as I should."* But in the early '70s I was stuck. I was still grieving the loss of Chandler, my adopted son was getting sick in a scary way and I was struggling with Pharaoh. My prayers didn't seem to be answered. Fortunately, through my participation in the Charismatic Communion of Presbyterian Ministers, I discovered Dick and Lois Adams. I heard they specialized in inner healing. I went to see Dick and Lois in San Diego. They took the time to hear me out and pray in an unhurried and conversational way. I told them my mental picture of my mother was of her screaming denunciations at me and slapping and socking me on the side of my face. They prayed Jesus would help me to relive such awful memories in His presence while they prayed He would heal my memories. I was comforted and encouraged, but nothing happened at that time. As we separated, I know they continued to intercede for me and I continued to pray for healing.

Then one day I was looking through an old family picture album. As I did so, I came upon my mother's graduation photo. In this picture my mother had a very pensive and wistful look. As I looked at it, the thought came to me, *"This is who she always wanted to be,"* but she had always been reacting to her mother who was neurotic, fearful and controlling to the max. Her mother was also a devout Christian and when my mother was angry she would pronounce her mother a hypocrite. As I looked at my mother's 18-year old face, something came over me;[53] I saw her sympathetically, struggling to be a better person and losing it despite her struggle. My heart softened and I began to forgive her. In time I fully forgave her, and on the way I became less of a beast.

It wasn't long before the Holy Spirit began to speak to me about my behavior towards my little sister Martha. She was born when I was ten. She was a cute baby girl and was delightful. Unfortunately, my mother felt it would be a good idea for me to be the babysitter. As I reached the age of twelve, my older sisters were usually not available; they were away at prep school and then college. You can imagine how much a 12-year old boy would enjoy coming home from school in order to take his baby sister a walk around the block, first in her

---

[53] This phrase is a good description of the Holy Spirit speaking.

stroller and later holding her hand. I was frustrated by this duty. I wanted to be playing with my friends instead of sitting with Martha at home. I'm ashamed to admit, but I began to do things to make my times with her unpleasant, to say hurtful things and to do things to scare her. Instead of my dear sister, she became my burden. Thank God, I don't think I ever hurt her physically, but I was mean.

In 1974 Martha came west with her husband. I had not seen her since I had performed her marriage some fourteen years before. She was a lovely Christian woman. I got her aside and asked her to forgive me for all of my meanness to her as a child. She said to me as she smiled, "Bobby I forgave you a long time ago. It's okay," and we embraced. Heaven came down and glory filled my soul.

My reflections about my behavior with Martha caused me to think even more about my childhood. I did not like what I remembered. I was skinny, was often sick, and I was temperamental. I was neurotically fussy about my room and belongings. I had throw rugs with tassels on the ends and was compelled to keep the tassels straight. My sisters loved to come in and mess them up so I would have to re-straighten them. My mother dressed me in nice clothes to go to school and I was always punished if I got them dirty or torn (those were Depression years where a penny saved was a penny earned). I did get in a few fights at school but I was bullied at times and too often a sissy. I was ashamed of my body, especially when we had to get undressed in the Jr. High locker room. I didn't like my curly, dark hair. I wanted straight blond hair like Georgie Knapp, who played quarterback. I was usually near the end when they chose up teams and being a "W" I would always be assigned to sit in the back of the class.

I made another appointment with Dick and Lois to pray for my self-image. They prayed a while. Lois said, "Lord, help Bob see himself the way You saw him as a boy." Suddenly I saw myself as though in a mirror as a boy nine or ten years old, smiling. The sight broke me. I wept uncontrollably. I was beautiful. My self-hate began to diminish, and with it, behavior that was hateful.

About two years later I realized I needed to deal with my teenage image. When I was in a rage my mother would say, "You're just like a bull in a china shop. Your nostrils dilate and you're snorting and ready to destroy everything in sight." That came in very handy in high school football. As a defensive end I made a lot of sacks and stopped a lot of end runs even though I only weighed 140 pounds. In my senior year we were undefeated. In our last game for the championship we were ahead by six points. Towards the end, we stopped the other team at the goal line and held them four downs. On the last down, I was offside, which gave them another chance. They scored and beat us. I was devastated. I kicked myself around the block for several years over that one. I could not forgive myself.

I heard about a man named Tony out in Covina. He was a former Marine and a fisherman. He was holding Pentecostal services in his home. He was known for his gift of the Word of Knowledge. I went with my friend Lyle to check him out. Toward the end of the meeting he looked at me and said, "You, sir, may I minister to you?" I was touched he noticed me. *"I'd be grateful if you would."* As I went forward to sit in the "hot seat" he said, "I see a bull." I thought, *"I'm in trouble now. He's going to flay me alive, but God knows I deserve to be whipped, so Lord give me courage to receive what he says."* He laid hands on me and prayed. He began by describing all of the good and wonderful things about a bull.[54] I was stunned. The prayer turned out to be an affirmation of all of the strengths that God had put in me. I went forward to be chastened, but I left feeling honored. I was seeing my assets more than my liabilities and it was liberating.

It's a good thing I was facing the roots of my anger because it was destroying my marriage. Twice in the early '70s Marilyn tried to leave me. She had had it with my irritability and need to control. Though she tried, she was never gone more than a day. She couldn't abandon the children and especially Sam in his growing need. We couldn't afford counseling so I sought for the answers in scripture. I began to come to terms with the facts of Romans 6:14, **"Sin will have no dominion over you, since you are not under law but under grace."** That gave me hope. I began to say to myself, *"I don't have to be angry, Jesus has provided victory over my anger."*

Soon thereafter I found a book called, "Do Yourself a Favor and Love Your Wife."[55] It was terrific. It really convicted me of what I had done to Marilyn. In early courtship and marriage, though I loved her dearly, I couldn't accept her exactly as she was. I had to make

---

[54] Bulls are known for their tremendous strength; they can pull a heavy load through rough circumstances. They endure against all odds. A fighting bull can whip a tiger.
[55] I forget the author's name.

her over into my image. I did appreciate and delight in her in many ways, but in too many I had to put her into my mold. She was a social person with lots of friends. I pressured her to get out of her sorority and drop some of her friends to have more time for ME. She was family centered, first of all with her family of origin, and then with our family. But I wanted her to break away to go to church meetings – especially prayer meetings – and revivals. She was a servant behind the scenes; she did the little things to bless people. I wanted her up front singing and testifying and helping me pray for others. You see what I was doing; I was sculpturing her to come into conformity with ME. I made her miserable. It came as a shock to me that I needed to let her be and accept her fully as she was. I was to notice all the good in her and celebrate it and be thankful instead of complaining.

There was another big thing the book did for me. It made me face my selfishness and self-centeredness. I used to come home (at Chandler and Glendale) with the attitude my home was my castle. I wanted to relax after a hard day. Figuratively speaking, I wanted to sit in my favorite chair with my feet up, watching my favorite program, while my adoring wife would bring iced tea and keep the children quiet. Meanwhile my wife was hoping I would come home early to settle Sam, get the sock out of the washer drain, fix the windowpane that Phil broke, and play with the children while she got dinner. The text that got me was, **"The Son of Man came not to be served but to serve, and to give His life as a ransom for many."** Mark 10:45.

I knew what I had to do. I had to deny myself and take up my cross daily for my wife and children.[56] I had been doing that for my church. But more sacrificial love was needed at home in terms of tender loving attention and care. I kept trying to do that, but anger and impatience would often sabotage my efforts. Then I would get into the Romans 7:14-25 striving to overcome my sin. The harder I tried, the worse I failed. I knew Jesus was the solution, but I was focused on the problem more than the answer. I needed to <u>see</u> by revelation that Jesus not only died for our sin, in our place, but also He died **to** sin as the representative head of a new humanity. In Him, on the Cross, we were cut off from the guilt **and** the **power of sin. "Our old sinful selves were crucified with Christ so that sin might lose its power in our lives. We are no longer slaves to sin. For when we died with Christ we were set free from the power of sin."** (Romans 6:6-7 NLT)

I needed to believe and count on the fact that when Jesus died on the Cross I died with Him to the power of sin. My old angry self died in Him. Then when He was buried, my own sinful self was buried too. (The burial emphasizes sin has no more claim on me.) When He rose from the grave triumphant over the world, the flesh, and the devil, I rose with Him triumphant over the dominion of sin. When He ascended into heaven, I was made to sit in the heavenly places with Him. This is the teaching of Romans 6:1-11, Galatians 2:20, 2 Corinthians 5:14, plus Ephesians 2:6.

That I had died to sin with Christ on the Cross was hard for me to believe because my behavior denied it.

---

[56] I must confess inside myself I was saying, *"But Lord, who will look after my needs?* I felt He said to me, **"Leave that to Me."**

81

There was a long up and down struggle to believe and receive what God has given in Christ. I was taught to confess victory over sin in Christ, and praise Him for it until it was a reality, and then praise Him even more. I've said it before – I'm a slow learner, but I prayed I might see what the Word of God says is true. At times I saw it clearly – at other times I was too distracted.

I found it essential to obey the rest of Romans 6 also – that means surrendering our members totally to Christ. I had done that after conversion, but found it necessary for a long time to do it every day by praying something like, *"O God, I surrender my will to do only Your will today, and my heart to love everyone as You do, my mind to think Your thoughts after you, my eyes to see everyone as You see them, my ears to hear Your word and obey it, and my mouth to speak Your words of grace and truth."*

One more thing: I needed to see, as Paul did in Romans 7, on the Cross I died with Christ to the law and was joined to Him. The law says, in effect, "Do, do, do; you haven't done enough, try harder to overcome, then you will be blessed." Jesus says, in effect, "I have already done it, overcome it, and <u>given</u> you the victory. Believe in Me, rely on Me, keep receiving My love and truth and you are fully blessed. Then do what my loving Spirit prompts you to do."[57]

Eventually Frank Laubach put me on to a hymn that has helped me enormously, "Dying With Jesus, by death Reckoned Mine."

---

[57] The Whitaker summary of Romans 6-8.

"Dying with Jesus, by death Reckoned mine;
Living with Jesus a new life divine;
Looking to Jesus til glory doth shine,
Moment by moment, O Lord, I am Thine.
Moment by moment I'm kept in His love;
Moment by moment I've life from above;
Looking to Jesus til glory doth shine;
Moment by moment, O Lord, I am Thine.

CHAPTER 13

Feeding the Hungry

In the winter of 1973 Rod Williams called me from Melodyland Christian Center[58] in Anaheim, CA. What a surprise. He had been teaching theology at the Presbyterian seminary in Austin, TX, but responded to Ralph Wilkerson's invitation to develop theological training for the converts of the Jesus People movement. Rod wanted me to be one of his teachers. He said, "Bob, what classes could you teach for us?" *I could teach pastoral care.* He said, "I'm sorry, that's already covered." *"Well, I could teach evangelism like I do at GPC."* He said, "I've got a man for that too." Then he said, "What about church history?" I said, *"Oh, Rod, I love church history but I've never taught it."*[59] He said, "Do you think you could get ready by September?" I knew I could, so I told him, *"If Pharaoh will let me*

---

[58] Melodyland had been a wonderful center for musical entertainment. It was just a stone's throw from the entrance to Disneyland. Pastor Ralph Wilkerson bought it and turned it into a thriving center of Christian outreach and worship. It became the place for the advancement of charismatic teaching and worship.

[59] At Yale I had the best church history professors in the world, Bainton and Latourette. They were both evangelicals.

teach on Saturdays, I will." So, I started cramming on church history.

Pharaoh did not like the idea. It would cut into my time and energy. I wouldn't be available for Saturday mornings. I pleaded; he said, "You'll have to take it up with the Session." I wrote up my proposal and we went to Session. Pharaoh made a strong case against it, but surprisingly, the Session voted substantially for me to be allowed to do it. That didn't help the tensions between Pharaoh and me. In late summer I took my family for vacation to the charming village of Cambria, CA, up near Hearst Castle. While they played, I crammed some more.

Then in September I met my first class at Melodyland on a Saturday morning. Was I ever excited! There were about twelve in the first quarter. In the next five years it would quickly increase to hundreds. By then the classes met on Thursday afternoons and evenings. These young people were mostly new converts ranging in age from eighteen to forty, from all walks of life and social strata. They were excited about Jesus and the Bible. It was just wonderful to see how they soaked up everything I could give them, study hard and write papers. Their stories were fascinating. I've never seen more highly motivated students. Every class began with fifteen or twenty minutes of worship. We always had talented instrumentalists who could lead worship. The singing and the prayers and the eager faces stoked me. I departed from the standard method of teaching. For each period of church history, and for the leading issues of the Christian movement, I selected key personalities and told their story with as much passion and interest as I could summon. My students loved it.

Many said, "I always thought history was boring, but not this class," and I became one of the most popular teachers at Melodyland.

In those days I was like a racehorse chomping at the bit and wanting to run. I was always trying to find a way out from under Pharaoh. I remember Brick saying, "Can't you just wait awhile?" I remember trying to persuade God to give me a green light to leave by the end of 1973. Barbie Danks[60] called me one day and said, "I woke up in the middle of the night and heard these strange words, 'Stay! You're not ready to move yet.' I wondered what that was about and you came to mind." Then she said, "I assure you, I do not lie awake at night thinking about you. I'm just supposed to transmit this word. Thank God, this doesn't happen very often."

By the winter of '74, a plan had begun to form. I would ask permission from my Presbytery to pastor the growing number of renewal prayer groups that were developing in the churches of Southern California. I would seek to help the new charismatics become a positive and unifying force for the renewal of their churches instead of repeating some of the mistakes we made at Chandler. By this time the outpouring of the Holy Spirit was at its peak nationally, and denominational and interdenominational conferences and seminars were abundant. Already I had been invited to speak to many church and Para-church meetings to interpret what God was doing by His Holy Spirit. I counseled with Brick about my proposal. I

---

[60] Her husband, Rev. Ed Danks, pastor of First Presbyterian Church Burbank, had befriended me and I helped him start a healing service.

told him I was on the verge of stepping out by faith and trusting God would provide for my family and me. I believed we could live on honorariums and gifts that would come from the enthusiastic participants in the movement. Brick had done this before me. He said, "Bob, the Lord always pays for what He orders. Just be sure this is what He is ordering and not just your proposal. Then your support will be provided." I prayed about this. It was scary for Marilyn not to have a regular salary and benefits. I believed if Pharaoh would give his blessing and Presbytery would accept my proposal, it would work.

So I shaved and changed my clothes and came before Pharaoh (Genesis 41:14). The plan seemed good to Pharaoh and all his officials (Genesis 41:37). However, he did not say, "Since God has made all this known to you, there is no one as wise and discerning as you" (Genesis 41:39).

Though the church gave me a terrific send off, I never really did leave Glendale Presbyterian. How could I? My family was deeply involved in the Sunday school and Youth Program. My wife was a Deacon, visiting the shut-ins and teaching Sunday school to kindergarten children. My daughters were meeting the youth leaders who would become their husbands. I was developing a midweek prayer group that would be instrumental in renewal and some of my financial supporters came from that church. I can never forget the marriage of my first daughter Emily to Dale Paulsen, a seminary intern. I took her down the aisle, stepped up on the platform and led the marriage service. Later it was the same with Laura who married one of the favorite GPC young men, Charlie Little, and we rejoiced with his parents who were in my Bible class. Amy's husband to be, Mike McClenahan, from Grandview Presbyterian, later became the Youth Minister at GPC.[61] As with my first two daughters, I married Amy and Mike in '85. We all still go back for reunions. Pharaoh left GPC in late '74 and I was privileged to have wonderful close relationships with the three men who followed him. They often had me as a speaker and teacher. Wonderful friendships and memories keep me tied to GPC.

---

[61] All of my daughters married Fuller Seminary graduates who became Presbyterian Ministers.

CHAPTER 14

Adventure in Faith

We became close to Dick and Lois Adams through their prayers for me, and joint ministry endeavors. Sometime in early spring of 1977, Lois suggested to Marilyn we could provide employment for their son by building houses at Lake Tahoe and then selling them. Their son Mike, who had recently graduated from a school for the deaf, could not find employment in construction due to his handicap. Marilyn got all excited about helping him. She knew him to be a wonderful young man deserving of our support.

Before I knew it, the Adams and Whitakers were on their way to Tahoe. I must say, I thought the whole thing was far out. I had never been to Tahoe. It was a nine-hour drive north of our home in Glendale and for the Adams it was eleven hours. I thought it would be far easier to build a cabin at Big Bear near Los Angeles. But then we arrived at Lake Tahoe. Even though I'd begun to travel the world, I had never seen anything so beautiful. Lois guided us to Tahoma and to two lots, side-by-side, selling for $3,000 apiece. They were small, but were shaded with lovely trees, some

100 ft. tall and 1/4 mile from the lake. I had all sorts of questions. How would I afford this; if I could get the money, how would I repay it; what if the houses didn't sell? Being a tightwad, this was huge.

Somehow faith arose in my heart. I thought to myself, *"Marilyn has followed me in my crazy adventures, it's time for me to let her take the lead. This is a mission of mercy. Somebody's got to believe in Mike. He's a big, strapping, intelligent and delightful young man. Surely he deserves our investment."* Next thing I knew we were in Mariani's real estate office. We were talking terms. We all decided to go for it. Dick and Lois selected blueprints for a nice conservative one-story cabin. I thought to myself, *"Well, if we're going to build a cabin we might as well make it big enough for my whole family,"* so I selected a charming 24x32 two story structure. We calculated that with Mike working for $5/hour[62] to do the foundation and framing, we could finish it out as a family for a total of about $30,000. At the same time it occurred to me I could get some of the working funds by borrowing on my insurance.

Within a week or two Marilyn flew back up to Tahoe and, with help from Mariani's assistant Bev, made the rounds of all the official government offices and obtained the permits to build our house and for all of the necessary inspections and utilities.

By May 20th Mike was underway. Lois and Dick were living in a trailer on site supervising and ordering materials while he built their house first. He was rugged and worked from 5:30 AM 'til dark. He found some neighbors to help him. Before long he had started

---

[62] Even in 1977 that was cheap. Mike had proposed that he work for minimal wages because he was a novice.

on our house. I remember taking my mother up to see it in July. I was astounded and said, *"Oh my dear, I had no idea this would be so big."*

That year Philip graduated from high school and went on an evangelistic mission to the beaches of Hawaii with Youth With a Mission. By mid-summer he came home and immediately joined Mike to finish the framing of our house.[63] (Philip had already spent several summers working in construction.) By mid-August through early September, our whole family, except Emily, went up and joined in the work. We stayed in rental houses and pretty much worked from dawn to dusk. We did take a little time off for fun. Mike had a powerful motorboat and delighted in taking us for wonderful rides all over beautiful Lake Tahoe. We all took turns skiing. Those were wonderful, happy times. I can still see Mike's face grinning from ear to ear as he revved up his hotrod motor. He couldn't hear it, but he loved to feel the vibrations and we would all egg him on.

We put the siding on the house and roofed it even though it was a steep A-frame style roof. By the time we left, the shell of the house was finished, windows were installed and the door openings covered with plywood for the winter. During the late fall I arranged for the electricity, plumbing and furnace to be installed. At Christmas and the following summer we continued as a family to finish the house. Emily and her husband Dale joined us. My children did all of the

---

[63] Working with Mike presented special challenges because of his deafness. He could speak but was often difficult to understand. If his back were turned, Philip would get his attention by playfully tossing a nail at him. Because he couldn't hear "Watch out!" twice he fell off the roof. Thank God no one was injured.

itchy insulation, helped me hang sheetrock and did all the plastering and painting, and eventually Amy and Marilyn wallpapered the bedrooms. Much of the furniture was homemade by Philip.

At some point before we finished the house, perhaps it was after I hung the outside doors, people started to come by and make offers. We had pretty much done the job for about $30,000, since all of our labor was free. Our first offer was for $40,000. Knowing I had to pay off my insurance, I wanted to sell as planned. But the beauty of Tahoe tugged at my heart and a plan was hatching in my mind to rent it out to skiers and vacationers so we could keep it as a vacation home for the family. The clincher was my children. Led by Laura they said, "No way, Dad, you can't sell it. Not after all the work we put into it." So their mean, stingy old dad gave in, I am happy to say. For thirteen wonderful years it was our vacation and holiday home, not only for us but also for my children's friends, spouses, children and our friends. The beauty of the lake, the smell of the pines and fir trees, the chatter of the Blue jays and the wonder of the High Sierra snows, captivated and relaxed us. This was a place of ever-fresh physical and spiritual renewal.

In the summer of '78 the Area Forrester informed me our two prettiest large trees were infested with bark beetles and would soon have to be cut down. I was sick about it. Those particular trees made a magnificent canopy over the entry of the house. I couldn't give them up. I remembered what Francis MacNutt did. All the elm trees on his street were dying. He put his arms around the two elms on his property and prayed for their healing. His elms survived, the others did not.[64] So, when no one was looking, I hugged my trees and prayed for them (more than once.) I am happy to say one survived another twelve years and the other survived until a few years ago. This experience proved to be very important. In later years, joined by my wife, on occasion we were able to save beautiful and fruitful trees from disease and death. One of our best friends owned several large commercial fruit orchards. One year he was on the verge of bankruptcy and told us if he did not have a good harvest he would go under. We volunteered to pray for his orchards and journeyed several hundred miles to pray over his trees. He had a bumper crop that year and survived.[65]

---

[64] Trees are living things. Experiments have been done that prove plant life respond to prayer.

[65] If you are interested, see Appendix G to see the kind of prayer we have found effective.

CHAPTER 15

Mourning to Dancing

I've mentioned Sam, who was born in 1967, and adopted by us before we left Arizona. As a baby he cried a lot; it also became apparent he was fearful and rebellious. We prayed for him to have a peaceful disposition, but he kept getting more difficult to care for and enjoy. At home and church he was disruptive.

At the age of four (1971) we noticed Sam's eyelids would flicker and he would briefly blank out. We took him to a pediatrician. An EEG proved he had Petit Mal (epilepsy). He was put on Phenobarbital and we increased our prayers and loving attention only to see the Petit Mal seizures increase in number and severity.

Before long Sam started having psychomotor seizures every day. His eyes would stare with a slight blinking of his lids; his arms and hands would extend in a jerking motion and he would sometimes stagger about and bump into things. These would last 20-30 seconds, during which time he could neither see nor hear. He had eight to twenty of these daily and sometimes thirty or more. This was dangerous – we had to forbid bike riding, skate boarding, swimming, etc. For his own safety he had to be watched. It was frustrating for him and for us. Tragically other children would tease or take advantage of him, which would lead to fights. Nevertheless, Sam had a great sense of humor and loved to play games. He was especially fond of baseball, and after we signed wavers, the YMCA allowed him to play and later he played in Little League. I remember him pitching and having a seizure on the mound and people in the stands looking on with bewilderment. As I watched him gyrating about the mound I wanted to hide. But he recovered and went on to pitch a good game.

From 1971 on the neurologists at UCLA tried all relevant anti-seizure drugs and combinations, but the seizures kept getting worse. They said his seizures were intractable. I'm not sure which was worse, the seizures or the drugs. The drugs had serious effects on his behavior. He was terribly hard to discipline and we received many unhappy notes from his teachers and were often humiliated by his behavior in public. Spanking was useless; he would just go berserk. We exhausted all of James Dobson's remedies.

One morning at breakfast Sam made a terrible sound, fell off his chair and hit the floor. He started to turn blue. Philip immediately scooped him up and ran to Dr. Borg's house 50 yards away and burst into his kitchen. Dr. Borg quickly attended to him. It was a mild Grand Mal seizure. This dreaded thing happened when he was eight. Thereafter he had one a week as well as 15-20 psychomotor seizures every day. I cannot understand how a human body can take a Grand Mal seizure. They are totally horrible. Sam's body would be slammed against the floor with awful shaking and contortions; his head would arch back until we feared his neck would break. His eyes rolled back until only the whites could be seen. He seemed to be strangling while gasping for air with horrible sounds. This would go on for one or two minutes, then he would go limp and expel saliva in bubbles. Afterwards he would sleep like a dead man for an hour and be wiped out for the rest of the day. Thank God, during the seizures, Sam did not know or feel what was happening.

Sam's brain was so scrambled by meds and seizures he couldn't cope with schoolwork. In fourth grade he was put in Special Ed. He would say to me, "Daddy, if God loves me, why doesn't He stop my wiggles?" I tried to explain that often God lets us go through trials to learn important lessons of faith, endurance and courage and we believed that somehow, someday, God would heal. We tried every diet, every herb and went to some of the best Christian healers in the country. At times we had seasons of prayer and fasting involving scores of people, but he kept getting worse.

Sam had a little parakeet that he adored. His name was Steve. This was his main consolation in all his suffering. One Saturday as Sam's sisters were cleaning, the birdcage was knocked over, the window was open and Steve flew away. Sam was furious at his sisters; his wailing and anger were extreme. He had often been upset, but this was nonstop. In the midst of it, I broke. I went upstairs and fell on my knees by my bed. I cried to the Lord, *"God, I cannot take this. I've seen him go from bad to worse; nothing works and now he's stripped of his last joy. I hope you enjoy watching it, because I can't take it anymore"*. I went on in that vein. All the while the still, small voice was saying, **"Trust me, Trust me."** *"Oh, yes, trust You. What new miseries do you have in store?"* **"Trust me, Trust me."** Somehow I said, *"Okay, I will trust You. I will trust You to bring Steve back."* I went downstairs and told Sam, *"Let's pray to God and ask Him to bring Steve back."* He prayed with me. Then we got everyone we could and went through the neighborhood calling for Steve until nightfall. We prayed for Steve that night because as a tropical bird they are not equipped for the cool night air. Sunday morning Sam wanted to continue the search but I told him we had to go to Sunday school and church, so we did. We came home. Sam went into his room, looked out his window and there in the camellia bush was Steve. He reached out his finger, Steve hopped onto it, and we all rejoiced in the Lord. Hope began to rise. If God could bring Steve back, maybe Sam could be healed soon.

Before long Ron and Diane Abarta came to see us. They were a young couple in our church with three small children. We had known them and loved them for some time and they had been Sam's Sunday school teachers. They told us they had been praying for Sam and believed that God wanted to heal him. *"We believe God wants to heal him also, but the question is when?"* Diane responded, "We believe the time is now." They then shared with us how some years before, God had baptized them in the Holy Spirit and they had several experiences of praying for the healing of persons and had seen good results. As they shared, it was evident to us that they were gifted in the Spirit. They had the gift of faith, of knowledge, of discernment, and of tongues and healing. We made plans for them to spend time with Sam. They were very wise. A few times they had him over to their house to play with their boys and their little dog, whom he loved. After they gained his trust, they began to ask him how he felt about what he was going through and prayed for him some. In late October 1977 we took Sam for an intensive time of prayer. Sam sat between them with the little dog in his lap. They explained to him that Jesus wanted to heal him and gently laid hands on him as they prayed. God gave Ron a vision of a baby in a tent and knives coming through the walls of the tent towards him.[66] He then understood this to mean that when Sam was a baby in his mother's womb, an abortion was attempted.[67] They continued to pray quietly for Sam in tongues. They then asked Sam to imagine himself as a baby in his mother's tummy. Before long, Sam cried out, "I'm scared." They then prayed that Jesus would come to Sam. In a little bit Sam reported that he could see the baby Jesus with him. Soon we all sensed the peace of the Lord and Ron was led to prophesy, "He will never have Grand Mal seizures again."

Soon it was evident that Sam's Grand Mal seizures had stopped and his psychomotor seizures were beginning to decrease. Sam continued to meet with the Abarta's for prayer and they continued to pray for the cessation of all seizures. By the end of January of '78 he was having very few psychomotor seizures. Meanwhile, we tapered him off his anti-seizure medicine. By Pentecost in the spring of '78, the seizures were gone![68]

---

[66] This is an example of the gift of the Word of Knowledge.

[67] We realize the vision could be interpreted differently.

[68] Subsequently we learned that Sam needed to continue taking one Depakene a day to prevent small Petit Mal incidents.

All through late '77 and '78 we were "like those who dream."[69] We had to pinch ourselves; the dread seizures were gone. We were praising the Lord. Sam could live a normal life – he could walk to school and back, he could explore the neighborhood on his bike and skateboard. In the winter of '78 he skied at Tahoe, raising his arms in victory. His Special Ed teacher said he was learning at a faster rate. Far and wide, in my preaching missions and our charismatic conferences and prayer rallies, we reported what great things the Lord had done. Faith was quickened for thousands – maybe tens of thousands. In those days testimony tapes were freely circulated; Sam's story went all over New Zealand resulting in speaking invitations.

I'm a slow learner. I don't know when it came to me, but like a revelation it awakened in me. Jesus had healed Sam through the gifts of the Holy Spirit (faith, knowledge, tongues, prophecy and healing were especially evident). The crucial encounter was October 30, 1977 at the Abarta's – that was the tenth anniversary of my dismissal by Phoenix Presbytery for refusing to renounce the gifts of the Holy Spirit!!

For me, that was like God was saying: **"I have not forgotten the price you paid to honor My gifts – now you truly know how precious they are."**

---

[69] Psalm 126:1b-2 "We were like those who dream. Our mouth was filled with laughter and our tongue with shouts of joy; then they said among the nations, 'The Lord has done great things for them.'"

CHAPTER 16

All Things are Possible

After Sam's healing, my faith was soaring – it had been rising on the winds of the Spirit for years. But the cessation of Grand Mal seizures, despite the doctor's declaration they could not be stopped, was awesome.[70] As Jesus said to the father of the epileptic boy, **"All things are possible for one who believes."**[71] At Chandler we had learned the power of the spiritual gifts when operating through a team ministry of strong faith. We had seen some healings through one-on-one prayer. But we saw more impressive healings of stubborn conditions when several people with different gifts took unhurried time to pray together in faith for a person. This was particularly true if we did so for three or four weeks with the laying on of hands. I remember one man whose emphysema was overcome in this way, and another who came to Chandler to die of serious heart disease and became a vigorous evangelist. (In

---

[70] The doctors at UCLA Neurological Center were some of the best in the world.
[71] Mark 9:23 ESV.

that case every one in the group felt a strong sensation of fire and heat generated by the Holy Spirit.)

As in the case of Sam's healing, we found the word of knowledge gift was very important in serious cases to discover the root of the problem. Also we found the gift of faith and anointed prayer and the healing gift would then improve or heal the malady. It's like in professional medical practice – correct diagnosis or an MRI is often needed to pinpoint the cause of the pain and hasten the treatment and cure.

We found praying out loud in tongues was usually more powerful than conventional prayer in the healing of all diseases and infirmities. I even did an informal survey of healers – they all agreed they saw more healings and more powerful healings after they started praying in tongues.

In exceptionally difficult cases the gift of discerning of spirits is a Godsend. Humanly speaking all seems well and, then in the presence of a gifted team praying, the sick person starts to react strangely and a spirit is detected. Whether the person is delivered then or later, the gift of wisdom is enormously helpful and praying in tongues is more powerful than one's native language to bring about deliverance.

So with fresh gusto I went to work to finish my part of a hopeful small book I was writing with a team of PCC leaders.[72] The book was intended to tell skeptics and inquirers that homosexuality can be healed through Christ by the power of the Holy Spirit. There

---

[72] I had proposed to the Board of the Presbyterian Charismatic Communion that we should write this book for all Presbyterian ministers and General Assembly Commissioners in time for the 78th General Assembly.

was strong agreement about writing this book; in all of the historic denominations there was a growing vocal minority who were saying homosexuality could not be healed – "they're born this way" – and "they should be allowed to be church leaders." All of the renewal groups in the denominations felt it was urgent we address this matter.

I finished my part of the book by mid-December '77. In late January I met up with Brick and we flew into balmy West Palm Beach, FL (only it was quite cold). Len LeSourd met us there and drove us to his gracious home in Boynton Beach to go to work finishing the book. Len's wife, Catherine Marshall, welcomed us with a warm hug as we entered their home. She chatted with us over a tasty and nutritious lunch.[73]

After lunch Len, Brick and I went across the street to their guesthouse and went to work reviewing, editing and rewriting some paragraphs of our book. We did this for three and half days until we felt the book was ready for the printer. In the evenings and over meals we enjoyed wonderful, stimulating fellowship with Len, Catherine and some of their family and friends. Following that, the whole Board came together at a nearby retreat center where we did more planning for the expanding work of PCC and prayed for the success of our book, "Healing for the Homosexual."

The book had basically three parts: the Biblical view of homosexuality; testimonies of healed homosexuals; and practical teaching about how to be made whole. Since the book is out of print, I'm going to share my own summary of the practical teaching because it is

---

[73] See Appendix H for more about Len LeSourd and Catherine Marshall.

even more needed today than it was then. Even more, the healing principles apply to any sinful tendency such as addiction to pornography, anger, gluttony, pride, alcoholism or drugs. All of us need to repent regularly of any besetting sin.

To be made whole we need to:

1. Focus on Jesus Christ as the One sent by God to show His love and to save and heal us. We need to meditate on a portion of the Gospels each day to awaken our faith in Him.[74]

2. Face the truth. All deeply rooted sin is hard to overcome. The first step is to face that God loves us, but He hates sin and warns of the consequences. He opposes all immoral and homosexual practices[75] and He condemns all hateful practices. He calls us to purity and forgiving love, and what He commands, He gives.

3. Admit we cannot conquer sin by ourselves. We need to receive by faith and prayer the loving and saving power of Jesus Christ <u>daily</u>.

4. Turn our sin and ourself over to God in a decisive prayer of surrender and confession of all of our sins and ask for forgiveness and cleansing. This is best done in the presence of a trusted Christian leader or group who will assure us we are forgiven in Christ and will keep us accountable and pray for us regularly. The regular confession of sins to a trusted counselor, relative or small group, and prayers for forgiveness with an attitude of repentance is essential for healing. **"Confess**

---

[74] See Appendix I, "How to Meditate on the Word."
[75] See Appendix J, "The Biblical Teaching on Homosexualty."

your sins to one another, and pray for one another, that you may be healed." James 5:16. We stress confession and accountability because it is necessary for the breaking of our pride and facing of uncomfortable truth. I never really faced my own worst sins until l told the truth to my wife or a trusted Christian brother; as I saw the hurt on their face I saw more clearly how awful my sin was in God's sight. That helped me to repent.

5. Learn to rely on the Word and grace of God to enable us to hate our sins, repent of them regularly and trust in God to give us the victory in accordance with His promises. Memorizing the following passages will help: Mark 8:34 **"If anyone would come after me let him deny himself and take up his cross and follow me,"** Romans 6, 1 Corinthians 10:13, Galatians 5, Ephesians 2:4-10, Ephesians 4:25-32, Ephesians 5:3-20, Ephesians 6:10-18. Please see Chapter 12, page 81.

6. Deal with the root causes of our sin. We have found our worst sins got started early in a hurtful relationship with one or both parents. Homosexuality often develops when a boy is regularly abused, abandoned or ignored by an uncaring father. The child begins to turn away from dad and starts to over-identify with mom.[76] In addition, there is the ever-present pressure of molesters.[77]

---

[76] Forty percent of American boys do not live with their dad.

[77] One out of three American children will be molested before their teenage years.

In inner healing prayer, we ask God to bring to mind the hurtful things that happened in childhood. We relive one memory at a time, asking Jesus to be present with us. We ask that He help us to feel deeply what we felt at the time of the hurtful incident. We ask Him to enable us to see the one who hurt us as He sees them and we wait in faith for Him to do so. We ask for grace to forgive and love that person as He does. We repent of bitterness and resentment towards the hurter. We ask to see Jesus healing us and to hear His words. This kind of prayer is best done with an experienced counselor or small redemptive group, but we can practice it alone. For a serious addiction this might have to be done regularly for at least a year.

7. Consider deliverance. In dealing with root causes, I believe that inner healing normally should precede dealing with demons. Quite often demons of hate, anger and unforgiveness leave quietly through inner healing. But where there is a persistent sinful passion or bondage that keeps us in a pattern of defeat and shame, we need to take authority over the devil and his demons. Jesus has given to all believers authority over the demonic. **"I have given you authority... over all the power of the enemy; and nothing shall hurt you."** Luke 10:19. **"These signs will accompany those who believe: in My name they will drive out demons."** Mark 16:17 NIV. Normally we can pray deliverance for ourselves unless we are seriously oppressed, i.e., we have practiced witchcraft, have been a psychic or

medium, have been in a coven or made a pact with Satan. In these cases we should seek an experienced ministry of deliverance.

Here are some ways we can pray deliverance for ourselves. "In the name of Jesus I command these lustful thoughts to leave." Or, "In the name of Jesus I take authority over you spirit of lust and I command you to go to the feet of Jesus and don't return." Another useful example, "You angry and judgmental spirit, get out and stay out in the name of Jesus." In connection with this, another example is given in Chapter 4, page 26. In these deliverance prayers we should speak out loud because normally the enemy does not know what we are thinking. After we have prayed deliverance for ourselves, we need to ask the Lord to fill us afresh with His Holy Spirit (see Luke 11:24-26). Of course, our own prayers may need to be fortified by the prayers of others or by a spiritual leader experienced in deliverance prayer.

8. Get involved in a believing and loving Christian fellowship or church where there is good Biblical teaching and vital worship. Contribute helpfully and unselfishly in every way we can. Make friends and find one or two we can be honest with and pray with. Learn to be an unselfish, loving and caring member of our own family and be like Jesus in sacrificial love toward our spouse.

9. Scripture warns us to avoid all evil influences: pornography, bars, suggestive TV programs, and any person or situation that tempts us to fall.

10. If we fall, remember the Lord Jesus is near at hand to lift us up, to forgive and cleanse us and to empower us to try again, with the expectation that complete liberation with all its joy, peace and love will eventually be ours. In basketball when we miss the basket we learn to rebound and make it on the second or third try. Confession to an accountability partner is more essential than ever.

11. First thing in the morning before we ruin the day, and last thing at night that we may sleep in peace, praise God with songs, hymns and spiritual songs, confess sin and ask for what we need. Learn to be a worshiper; die to the self-centered "I" -- get wrapped up in our wonderful Father God.

CHAPTER 17

When We All Get Together

I was wonderfully fortunate to be invited to participate in marvelous renewal conferences all over the United States and in many parts of the world. I went with stimulating Christian companions and had the adventure of discovering beautiful places. And to think, I had the privilege of being paid as a speaker in some of the most glorious gatherings of the saints!

One of the most memorable was my three-week trip to South Africa (January '80). I flew from Los Angeles to New York with Larry Christenson. Then as we changed planes I had time to visit with my new grandson, Andrew. At the time Emily and Dale were serving at the Presbyterian Church in Darien, CT. They brought baby Andrew so I could enjoy him and I delivered goodies from Nana. Then we flew on to Johannesburg, a sixteen-hour flight. I couldn't get over the fact that the renewal group in South Africa was bringing fourteen speakers from overseas to join an equal number from their country for the renewal conference. Then they housed us in what must have been a four-star hotel, The Landdrost,[78] and rented Milner Park for the venue. My room was on the sixth floor overlooking a lovely park full of flowers and my next-door neighbor was Larry Christenson.[79]

I taught two seminars. The first was on handling conflict. I told the story about Mr. Frasier at Chandler. As things got heated up at the Chandler church and people were agitating against my innovative ministry, old Mr. Frasier came to see me at my office. I can see him now as though it was today. He tapped on the door, I said, *"Come in."* There he stood in a Stetson hat, a pinstripe suit and tie, and if you will believe it, spats and cane. I invited him to sit down. As he removed his hat and sat down he said, "Mr. Whitaker, if I may be so bold, I came to give you some advice. As you know some are speaking out against your ministry and naturally you are under pressure to fight them. I would remind you of our Savior and how He conducted Himself when He was under trial and faced with all manner of false accusations. He never defended Himself. Remember that you are a sheep; you have no fangs or claws with which to fight. You have to rely on the Shepherd to defend you and protect you. Don't pay too much attention to your opposition. Go on with your preaching and counseling and keep speaking the inspired Word with love." We chatted about that and then he bid me good day and left. I found it to be the best advice I ever received. As the attacks mounted and the gossip increased I was greatly comforted to know I

---

[78] I have never seen the likes of their fruit buffet. They had all the fresh fruit that we have plus a huge variety of tropical fruits and it was delicious.

[79] See Appendix K for more about Larry Christenson.

was just to love everybody and speak the truth as the Spirit led.

The other seminar I taught was "Opening Up to the Holy Spirit." I was in for a surprise. There was a Black pastor from Durban. At home he had had a vision concerning this conference in which he saw a particular building he had never seen before. Then he saw a cavernous room, where I would be teaching the seminar, his seat, a crowd of people in the room, and saw the Holy Spirit coming down upon him and being baptized and speaking in tongues. Inspired by this vision he arranged to travel to the conference, came to Milner Park, saw the building from his vision, went in and went to the exact chair he had seen and sat down. Later on when I prayed for him the Holy Spirit came in power as in the vision. If there had been a mandatory registration fee, he probably would not have been able to come.

A charming man and his wife came to see me. We sat down over tea and cookies in the speakers lounge. The man had been heavily involved in a homosexual lifestyle. It was killing his marriage but his wife prayed faithfully for him for ten or twelve years. He finally was healed as he read and put into practice the well-known book, "Prison to Praise," by Merlin Carothers. Over the course of time he evolved a counseling and prayer ministry to gays that became an official ministry of his local Dutch Reformed Church. It was so encouraging to see he was doing what our book "Healing for the Homosexual" taught.

The conference was noteworthy for three reasons. There were a number of outstanding prophecies that the '80s and beyond would be a time of extraordinary evangelism of the continent of Africa. I'm pleased to say, and we have all witnessed, that since that time the evangelism of Africa and the growth of churches has been extraordinary.[80] The second noteworthy thing was the remarkable words of Everett (Terry) Fullam in his plenary address.[81] "The same Spirit who breathes life and renewal, also breathes death upon everything that is not of God." "We are in days of renewal but everywhere I go I see massive evidences of death … all of the renewal put together is not stemming the tide in the churches." Then he said, "Don't be surprised if things collapse around you … don't hold up your hands in horror. I think God is at work in our church. He is letting the fruit of evil seed collapse before our very eyes. Our church has tried everything to revive itself, except the gospel … God is allowing the fruit of what we have sown to bear the death that was implicit in it right from the beginning." Summing it up, Terry said, "Jesus made that unforgettable statement. He said, '**Every tree that my Father has not planted will be uprooted.**'"

These words comforted me with a more Godly perspective – I had been troubled that our renewal prayer groups were gradually diminishing, particularly where the local pastor was unsupportive. Also, despite 10% of our ministers being impacted by the renewal and despite frequent inspiring and equipping conferences almost everywhere, the denominations were sinking. They were declining in faith, morality, mission and

---

[80] Christianity grew ten times faster than the population growth in the last two decades of the Twentieth Century. Timothy Keller, "Kings Cross," Pg. 124.
[81] "New Vision" magazine, March-April 1980.

attendance. Terry helped me to see maybe it wasn't my fault after all.

The third noteworthy thing about our African conference was that it was a demonstration to all of Africa of unity through Christ. It had been planned strategically and financially so that 7,000 poor and rich, Black and White, Pentecostal, Catholic and Protestant could come together. At the worship services and in the fellowship and meal times there was marvelous interaction. I, myself, was able to grow closer to great leaders I had long known and admired, i.e. Loren Cunningham the leader of Youth With a Mission and Derek Prince, whom I have spoken of before, and Terry Fullam the Episcopal leader, etc.

After the six-day conference we went on a three-day retreat with the African leaders. It was a time of hearing about the tensions and difficulties they were working through as Apartheid was breaking up and there were new relationships forming. We also heard about the hurts and resentments that had developed during the long period of oppression and the hopes they had for their country. We spent a lot of time praying with them for healing and reconciliation and for evangelistic plans for the continent.

After the retreat we all scattered to itinerate throughout South Africa and preach in churches of our particular denominations. I was driven to Pretoria for meetings, and then flown to East London, then to Durban and back to Johannesburg. I was struck by how beautiful South Africa is. The flowering trees and bushes are gorgeous; the colorful birds are striking; I loved the early tropical mornings with light coming at 4:30 AM and the birds like a divine chorus. Those were great times to walk and pray. My last meeting was in a place called Benoni at a large Presbyterian church. As I had done many times before I told the story of how the Lord healed Sam through the gifts of the Holy Spirit. Many people were moved to tears. I flew away to home on a night flight loaded with presents for my family.

CHAPTER 18

Silverlake

It was a beautiful sunny day in late August 1980. We were vacationing in our little cabin at Lake Tahoe. The phone rang. It was Bob Raisbeck from Silverlake Presbyterian Church in the NE corner of Los Angeles. I knew Bob fairly well as a leader representing that church at Presbytery. He said, "Bob, as you probably know, Peter[82] is gone and we would like you to come and supply our pulpit and then maybe you would consider being a temporary interim pastor." I was pleased to hear from him. I had periodically ministered at the Silverlake church under Peter's ministry and I liked it. I told Bob we'd pray about it and get back to him in a few days.

When I phoned back I explained to Bob I would love to preach for them but about half of my Sundays were already committed. However, we made some changes and by October I was serving half time as the temporary interim pastor. I was still leading the

---

[82] Peter Hinstzoglou was an old friend who had served the Silverlake Church since 1970 and then accepted a call to Fallbrook Presbyterian Church in 1980.

Wednesday prayer and praise group at GPC and was still the Western representative of the Presbyterian Charismatic Communion with an itinerant ministry, but the truth was I needed to settle down in my own church for my family's sake.

During the fall of '80 I made a pleasant discovery. There was a vital core of people at Silverlake who wanted renewal and they were eager to work with me. They had been well taught by Peter, had a prayer chain and once a month they had a Sunday night prayer group that was unique. John Zeigler would have each person share what God had been doing in their lives over the past month and how He had answered their prayers. Then he put a chair in the middle of the room and asked anyone who wanted prayer to sit in the chair. Some of the others would then gather around them, lay hands on them and pray for their prayer need. This group was vital and full of faith. Some of them told me flat out, "You're supposed to be our new minister." I hoped that this was true. Meanwhile I decided to test the church. I would preach the strongest and most provocative sermons I knew and see how they responded. If they didn't like it, the interim thing would be over. If they did like it, we could go places together.

Those first Sundays I preached as powerfully as I could on faith in Jesus Christ and the miracle working power of God. Not only that, but we had altar calls. In most Presbyterian churches that's a no-no, but after the Benediction I would invite all those who wanted prayer for whatever cause to come forward and receive it with the laying on of hands. This was an enormous change. Presbyterian ministers are supposed to go to the rear door and shake hands with everybody as they leave. But they all seemed to roll with the punch. The most important thing about that church was that there was a lot of love among the people. They greeted each other with hugs and kisses. "Love covers a multitude of sins." 1 Peter 4:8.

Love flowed in the family, too. Emily and Dale moved back from Connecticut to Malibu.[83] On days off Nana and I could enjoy grandson Andrew, and within a year, baby Daniel.

Our worship service was at 9:30. Within three months I felt led of the Spirit, and the elders agreed, that we should have a teaching and sharing time at 11:00. So I commenced gathering the willing learners in the large upper room. I would give fifteen minutes of teaching from the Sermon on the Mount and from the strong passages like, **"If any man would come after me, let him deny himself, take up his cross and follow me."** Mark 8:34. Then I would break them into small clusters of two or three to discuss the meaning of the teaching for their own lives and ministries. Then we would come together to share as a group what the Lord was saying to us. The preaching and teaching times caused the people to face their shortcomings and sins and to seek the Lord at a deeper level.

Those early days at Silverlake were beautiful and exciting, but precarious. Behind the scenes a kind of high stakes game was going on. The Presbytery of San Fernando was okay with my being the interim minister but most of the power structure was negative about my becoming the permanent pastor. Since I had come

---

[83] Dale became the Assistant Pastor at Malibu Presbyterian Church for four years.

to the Presbytery twelve years before, the feeling was, "Whitaker should never be allowed to have his own church again." Pharaoh had confirmed that feeling to the leaders. That was also the attitude among the five Los Angeles area Presbyteries. If I wanted to minister in any church or start a renewal prayer group, I had to have the permission of the Presbytery with oversight of that church. I had had to meet with the Ministerial Relations committees of each Presbytery to get their permission and each time I had been grilled concerning my intentions, my methods and my message. The most commonly asked question was, "Why do you want to be a Presbyterian minister? Why don't you join a Pentecostal church?" I would say to them, *"I was raised a Presbyterian. I was ordained by Philadelphia, the mother Presbytery. I was a national missions pastor and like all the presbyters (elders) in scripture, I believe in all the gifts of the Holy Spirit."*

I had several meetings with the San Fernando MR committee. They were willing for my interim ministry to be extended but were most anxious that I not disclose my interest in becoming the permanent pastor. They made it clear the church would first have to conduct a full search for other qualified ministers before they would be allowed to consider me. They also said that since I was an interim I could not be a candidate for the permanent minister until I had gone away for a period of six months while the church looked at other candidates.[84] So I served eighteen months as the part time interim and then had to go away for half a year. Thank God I had my traveling ministry to sustain my family during that time.

---

[84] This was normal Presbyterian law.

February 8, 1983 was showdown time. The whole Presbytery was to meet at Silverlake Church to vote on whether or not they would allow me to accept the call of Silverlake to be their pastor. It was anyone's guess as to whether or not the power structure would prevent my acceptance. Fortunately, because of my ministry in many of the churches of the Presbytery, many of the presbyters were friends and supporters. They packed the meeting and I was voted in as the three quarter time pastor.[85] It was a great day. It was particularly great because some of my former opponents swung over and voted on my side.

How fitting it was to cap that success with a family celebration. On February 12th we all went to San Jose, California, for the wedding of my son Philip to Anne Slater at her home church, Westminster Presbyterian. In this case I did not officiate as at my daughter's weddings, but Phil and Anne's college pastor did the honors. It was a great celebration; I can see still Phil in his tailored grey suit.

---

[85] At my request I wanted to keep one quarter of my time for traveling ministry to encourage renewal of the Holy Spirit in the churches worldwide.

CHAPTER 19

Going Back

In the early winter of 1982 I picked up the phone, "Hi Mr. Whitaker, its Carrie Harter. I know it's been a long time since we've seen each other but I'm a big girl now[86] and I'm engaged to Casey Rice. We want you to come and perform our marriage on June 5th." In my mind I was starting to panic. *"Oh no, I have said to myself I will never go back. That church will never see my face again – But how can I say no to Carrie?"* Collecting my thoughts I said, *"Carrie, that's just wonderful that you're going to get married and very sweet of you to think of me, but I'll need time to pray about it. I'm very busy."* "Well Mr. Whitaker we would really appreciate it if you could find time." *"Well maybe, but Carrie I doubt the elders would be willing to allow me to conduct a marriage in that church."* She quickly replied, "My father (who was an elder) has already taken care of that. You're invited to come back and do the ceremony." Then in my mind, *"Oh dear, now what*

---

[86] Carrie lived across the street from our family in Chandler. She was a playmate of my children. Her parents were dear friends and had never consented to my ouster from the Chandler church.

do I say?" So then I said, *"Well you know Carrie, I don't ever do a marriage unless I do extensive premarital counseling beforehand."* "We anticipated that and Rev. so-and-so at Gilbert (the nearest town) has offered to do the marriage counseling for you." I said, *"Well that's very thoughtful of you. Okay I'll pray about it and get back to you in a few days."*

As I got off the phone I felt as if the still, small voice must have been saying, **"You turkey, you know what you ought to do. This is the child of your wife's best friend in Chandler."** My thoughts were this: I had always said that I had forgiven the people of Chandler Presbyterian for what they had done to my elders and me. I really believed that. But I had also made a vow never to go back. This was the kind of thing that we often ran across in our counseling with people and helping people to forgive those who have hurt them. When we are hurt so often we make a vow that is basically a vow of bitterness and pride. The vow is like, "They will never see my face again," or "See if I ever have anything to do with them again." We have found that these kinds of vows have gummed up the spiritual heart life of millions. I recognized this right away. I realized for my own spiritual health I had to renounce that vow in the Name of Jesus. There and then I said to the Lord, *"I'm not going to sweat it. Here and now I renounce my vow in the Name of Jesus Christ and I will go back to the church that threw me out and I'll trust You to enable me to love and forgive them face to face and to have a wonderful wedding with Carrie and Casey."* Of course Marilyn was happy.

June 4th I took most of my family back to a very hot Chandler, AZ. Saturday the 5th, the day of the wedding, I went in the office to clear signals with the leaders concerning the details of the wedding ceremony and, even though the two leaders were some of my old enemies, everything went well. I still remember what it was like to walk in the side door to the chancel and stand before the congregation to await the arrival of the groomsmen and bridesmaids and the bride. As I looked out over the congregation, there they all were, the people who had voted me out. A little grayer, a little older and mellower. I felt no hostility. I was engulfed with love. I felt the presence of God as strong as I've ever felt it in my life. As the groomsmen and bridesmaids came forward I was in another world. Then I refocused on Carrie who had grown up to be a lovely, blond, blue-eyed bride. As she came down the aisle smiling at Casey, I knew that all of heaven was smiling upon us and I was wrapped up in His love and grace. It was as though heaven kissed us all.

After the ceremony, a beautiful reception was held in the churchyard in the 103-degree heat! I didn't mind it. I greeted every one of my former opponents with hugs and warm conversation. There was much laughter and tears and I did not detect any note of bitterness or hard feelings. We were all awash in God's love.

On the flight home I heard as clearly as I have ever heard anything, **"Thou preparest a table before me in the presence of mine enemies; thou anointest my head with oil; my cup runneth over."** Psalm 23:5 KJV. I choked up and wept.

Carrie and Casey Rice moved away to Texas soon thereafter. They had a fine family of three boys. About fifteen years later we learned that Casey was killed in an automobile accident and Carrie was left to raise the boys alone as a schoolteacher.

I'm very glad I went back.

CHAPTER 20

Top Priority

When we went to Silverlake the Lord impressed upon me I was not to start anything or change anything until I had prayed about it thoroughly. Also I knew I needed to be praying regularly with others who felt the same. Through the years I had learned prayer was top priority. In my first seven years of ministry I felt my life and ministry were mainly dependent on energy, thoughtful imagination and hard work. But I made a discovery. Prayer is more important than thinking and doing. It doesn't take time – it saves time when we pray first thing in the day. Seeking His direction, wisdom and power saved time in wasted motion over poor priorities, misunderstanding, and frustrating delays. It makes sense, doesn't it? If I tune into the mastermind of the universe and talk things over with Him and listen to Him things will go better.

Before I came to the conviction of the priority of prayer, life was like Murphy's Law – whatever could go wrong did go wrong. Afterwards, prayer proved to be like oil poured out on the rusty machinery of my life, making it run smoother and mesh better with others and producing more of worth. At home we found that prayer before meals helped to dampen contention between five strong-minded children and their parents, and unhurried prayer time before Session and committee meetings saved endless hassles, division and fruitlessness.

In my early years I had wrestled with the seeming conflict between the message of grace, where God gives generously, and the imperative of prayer that involves time and effort. The text of James 4:2 arrested me, **"You have not because you ask not."** (KJV) I knew from my experience that much is given freely by a gracious God, i.e. the sun, the rain and opportunities, but much must be asked for in specific prayer. There are many treasures of His grace that are only received through focused prayer, i.e. healing for a particular illness. God drew my attention to the literal meaning of James 5:16b – **"Strong enough for much is the prayer of a just man when energized"** (or when it is energizing) -- in other words, **prayer has much force in it's working**. Like radar, electricity or laser beams, prayer is a dynamic creative energy for enormous good. "Prayer is the most powerful form of energy that one can generate. The influence of prayer on the human mind and body is as demonstrable as that of the secreting glands. Its results can be measured in terms of increased buoyancy, greater intellectual vigor, moral stamina and a deeper understanding of human relationships."[87]

The second most important lesson I learned about prayer over the years is that it is an incredible

---

[87] Dr. Alexis Carrel, winner of the Nobel Prize for his work in physiology.

adventure and privilege to work together with God to accomplish His will. In answer to the question, "Why has God established prayer?" Pascal answered, "God has established prayer in the moral world in order to communicate to His creatures the dignity of causality."[88] This is a wonderful insight, God has chosen to make us cooperators with Him in all that He gives and does. This is very humbling and mind-blowing. Thus, God gives food, but we must cooperate and work with nature to grow it in order to have it. God also gives understanding, but we must apply our minds to observation, study and testing in order to receive that knowledge. In the same way, God gives marvelous promises of golden spiritual fruit, but we must reach out and pluck them by the hand of prayer. God's resources are like the giant city reservoirs of water;[89] prayer is like laying out the aqueducts, canals and pipes to channel that water to our living needs.

The third lesson I learned over the years is that prayer is an awesome responsibility; every bit as much as any work contract I might assume. I found through sometimes-bitter experience that if I failed to pray faithfully for some of the neediest people in my congregation, the consequences were grievous. "But does God rest my neighbor's good on our prayers?" we may ask, shrinking from the burden of so great an obligation. Why should we doubt that God imposes such a burden of love? God rests our neighbor's good upon our toil and thought. Why not upon our prayers? But

---

[88] "Lord Teach Us to Pray," pg. 6, by Alexander Whyte, Baker Book House
[89] Silverlake Presbyterian Church is directly across the street from a reservoir of water for the city of Los Angeles.

would not God give good gifts in any event? Apparently there are some gifts that God chooses to give through love's labor – prayer. God is intent on the growth of the comradeship. He has so ordered our days that we live in mutual reliance. He yearns to see the beloved community fulfilled on earth. Therefore, He has made us one life. We must not fail those whose welfare depends upon our toil, our thought – and prayer."[90]

The fourth lesson I learned about prayer is God gives to simple childlike faith, but faith is often shown in patient and persevering looking and waiting for the gift to arrive in God's time. The mystery of prayer is that when we engage in it we never know whether the answer will come sooner or later or both. In some things I have been astounded how quickly God has answered and in other things, as in the case of a very troubled person, the answer has taken years. I have learned not to quit until God basically says, **"Enough."**

At Silverlake the weightiest praying I did was with a small intercessory group. We met weekly at the home of Florine – an old prayer warrior. Mary, my secretary, was normally there and later there was Jan and Joy. We waited on the Holy Spirit to impress upon us our objectives and, as we prayed for these things over the years, they were achieved. The most important was the renewal of worship. We had a very good choir led by Eloise. It became a truly anointed choir. It was like the Lord Himself was singing through them. Later we developed a band. At the time such a thing in our kind of church was practically unknown. The band led inspired praise at the second, contemporary, service. I used to kid Chris, the drummer, and say *"You ought*

---

[90] "Prayer," pg. 112, by George Buttrick.

to go on the program, 'What's my Line?' They will never guess you are a drummer in a Presbyterian Church."

Another major objective was reaching young adults. When I went to Silverlake in 1980, Sam called it the "grandma church" because three fourths of the attendees were older women. As the church was renewed through preaching and prayer and small groups, young men started to come. The first ones were prayed for that they might stay. Soon many others followed. After about five years at least half of the attendees were young adults.

Another major objective was for healing. The whole church would get involved praying for persons who were sick, hospitalized or needed to have surgery. It was just amazing how our people would emerge from the sick rooms and hospitals radiant with new health. One of the most memorable was Dr. Boyajian. He had a herniated disc in his lower back. Two of us prayed for him with the laying on of hands. He felt something happen. Upon further testing he discovered that he was completely healed. He did not announce it until a year later and it had a powerful effect on the faith of our congregation. There were many healings of all types.

Another major objective was for teachers and leaders and for harmony. We never seemed to lack for good people to carry responsibility in all areas of the church's life, and Silverlake was and continued to be a loving family.

Little did I know how much we would need prayer.

In 1984 an awful blow fell on our family. My wife learned on the first Friday of December that she had breast cancer. I was staggered. We came home from the doctor like people in shock. We always communicated well, but we didn't know what to say to each other. I was hoping for peace and quiet and a time to gather my thoughts. I had forgotten I had an appointment – who should appear with a big smile on his handsome face but Mike McClenahan, Amy's boyfriend. He was all excited and spilled out to me his desire to marry Amy. He wanted my permission to propose to her. I was so in grief over Marilyn's condition, the first words out of my mouth weren't very good. I said, *"What makes you think she'll say yes?"* I don't remember what he said, but within a few weeks he proposed to her on the beach at Malibu.

So while Amy brought excitement and the joy of wedding preparations to our home, Marilyn went into surgery. I remember my thoughts as I sat in the little waiting room at St. Joseph's Hospital in Burbank. I was thinking and repenting of all the times I had hurt her and been inconsiderate. But I was also grateful for all the good. I was grateful we had been faithful to each other through all our ups and downs. I was very grateful our marriage had been renewed in a memorable mission trip to New Zealand in 1980.

As she began radiation treatments and then the painful process of chemotherapy, it was hard to see her being wasted. She was courageous, and needed to be, because she was very much engaged in all the preparations for the wedding in spite of her declining energy. We both were strengthened tremendously by our faith. As always, we knew the Lord was with us and would turn the difficulties into good and sorrow into joy. The wedding came seven months after her diagnosis. It was a huge gathering at Mike's family church, Grandview Presbyterian. In addition to my family, my parents and all of my sister's families came from the east. It was gratifying to see Mike's church and my church pitch in together and do all the catering beautifully. As mentioned before, I officiated. I felt transported by the love of God in Christ. Thanks be to God He has granted us moments that mirror the wedding joy of heaven.

CHAPTER 21

Release to the Captives

I've always loved the celebration of Easter. From childhood I knew it was special. The front of the church was filled with white lilies, the music was triumphant and it always had to be that way in my churches. I was never satisfied unless the sermon was convincing about Jesus' resurrection and also about ours. After I preached a message on the resurrection of Jesus Christ, I would say to the congregation something like, *"I know that some of you are here to please a family member, and we are delighted to have you. Perhaps you are indulgent about our belief in the resurrection, but you don't buy it. Perhaps you consider yourself an agnostic or even an atheist, but I want to suggest to you a 30-day experiment.*[91]

1. *Each morning take five minutes to read a small portion of one of the Gospels.*
2. *Before reading say, 'God, if You really are there, and if You really are what Christians say you*

---

[91] I think I learned it from Reg Goff, a Methodist minister famous for his prayer revivals.

are, please make Yourself known to me through the reading of this Book, which is supposed to be from You.'

3. *After reading a portion, try to put into practice what seems to speak to you.*

4. *Do this for thirty days and you will discover the Lord becoming real to you.[92]"*

One such Easter Sunday sitting before me in the front row was Diana Marchesi, a bright lawyer and one of my elders. Next to her was her lawyer husband, Scott, who rarely came. When he heard this challenge he said to himself he was going to prove me wrong.

Diana kept me apprised. Scott faithfully, morning by morning, would speak to God as I suggested, would read a small portion of a Gospel and seek to put into practice what spoke to him. Somewhere around the 25th day, Scott called me and asked to get together with me. I met with him as quick as I could. He said, "In addition to following your experiment I was also reading to my son Christopher, C.S. Lewis' 'Narnia Tales.' Something strange is going on. I can't get the Lion out of my head. I set out to prove you wrong, but it seems the Lion has got me." It was not long before Scott confessed his faith in Christ before the whole church and publicly told his story of coming to faith. Eventually he, also, became an elder.

I think of another young couple. The wife was a graduate student. She and her husband were very faithful participants in our second, contemporary, service. They also attended our mid-week praise and

---

[92] In all my years of ministry I have never seen this experiment fail if a person sincerely does it.

prayer time. He came to me one Sunday at the end of the service. He said, "I know you probably think that I'm one of your faithful Christians, but the truth is, I'm a hypocrite." Later we met in my study. I asked him to tell me his story. He told me that accidentally he came upon a pornographic magazine and was hooked. He had become a consumer of pornographic magazines and videos. He confessed it was destroying his marriage with his lovely wife. As usual, I was praying behind the scenes asking the Holy Spirit to lead and show me how to help him.

As I often do, I said, *"Tell me about your father."* He told me, "My father is an adulterer. He broke my mother's heart. He left and divorced her years ago. I have had nothing to do with him ever since." I then explained to him that he needed to face the fact he was doing the same thing as his father, only in a different way. He was able to see that. I then said, *"We are bound to repeat the behavior we hate in our parents until we forgive it."* He responded, regretfully, by saying, "Then I guess I can't be helped." I said, *"Yes, you can be helped. Let me pray for you that the Lord will break the hardness of your heart and give you grace to forgive your father."*

I then led him in the following kind of prayer; *"Father in heaven, I pray today that You will come to Tom and take him back in his memory to a time when things were good between him and his dad. Help him to relax and wait on You."* Then I waited in silence until he said, "I'm remembering going fishing with my dad." So I continued in prayer, *"Father, help him relive that fishing experience vividly. Help him to see it, hear it, and remember how he felt. Help him to relax and enjoy it and as he does so, help him to see his dad in the light of Your love."* Then I said to Tom, *"You know Jesus loved to get in the boat with His disciples and He is eternal. Ask Him to get in that boat with you and your dad and to enable you to see your dad the way He sees him and forgive him."*

Tom emerged from that inner healing prayer with a new ability to begin to forgive all that his dad had done. I then instructed him to continue to ask the Lord for memories and for the Lord to walk through those memories with him and give him a new perspective on his wayward father and thoroughly forgive him.

A week or two later we met again. He had made real progress in forgiving his dad and I encouraged him to pray about finding a way to reach out to him and begin the process of being reconciled. I also instructed him in how to reprogram his imagination, which had been taken over by lust. I taught him to take a paragraph of the Gospel of Mark each morning, to read it as a love letter from the Lord and to vividly picture it in his imagination and as much as possible to see himself there. *"Be the person who was being ministered to by Jesus; see Jesus and imagine His healing love penetrating your whole body and mind; hear His truth, calling you to obedience and the knowledge of God."* I asked him to renounce, in my presence, any pornographic media and promise to live in the scriptures every day with his imagination. He responded affirmatively.

I met with him several more times. He said, "You know, it's funny, but sometimes what begins as an exercise of my imagination has a life of its own. It seems like the video keeps running and Jesus is right here with me speaking to me." It was not long before Tom's marriage was renewed and he had learned how to stay clean before the Lord.

Whenever I think of our mid-week service, I remember Mary Ann. She was not a member of our church; she was a Catholic woman who loved to come. She was responsive and radiant with the light of God on her face. She was so genuinely happy and enthusiastic it was contagious. She had a neighbor named Dick. Like so many in the Silverlake community, he was gay and he was HIV positive. She befriended him and began to witness to him. At first he resisted her. He told her he was a member of the Metropolitan Community Church and one of the trustees. But he was captivated by her kindnesses and intrigued by the evident joy of the Lord in her. All the while she was praying for his salvation. Before long he was arrested on a morals charge involving a minor. He was desperate to find help. He called a counselor on the 700 Club; blurted out his story and asked for prayer. He experienced Christ cleansing him of all sin and giving him a new mind and heart. Immediately he called Mary Ann and told her of his conversion and started coming to our church with her. Mary Ann was a sister and mother to him as he went through a 30-week seminar to be healed of homosexuality. Many of us prayed with her for his wholeness. He became an enthusiastic participant in our fellowship, renounced the gay lifestyle and joined our church. Soon thereafter he discovered he had AIDS. He was a commercial artist and his business opportunities became fewer and fewer. Over and over again, despite his failing health and finances, he expressed his gratitude for the saving love of the Lord and our ministry to him.

In early 1986 a hippie couple, Pat and Alicia, showed up for the first time. During the sharing time (which we had at both services), Pat stood up to thank God. He had won at poker the night before the exact amount of a week's tithe and said he would be contributing it to the church that morning. Some laughed, and I said, *"Well the devil's had that money long enough."* Pat and Alicia had an interesting background. She was living with a guy who was a drug dealer. She would deliver the drugs all over the Hollywood Hills in her Porsche. Pat was her pool cleaner. Eventually she ran off with him and they got married. When they came to Silverlake they were new believers but not yet fully committed.

They lived in an old apartment atop several old garages. Their home was a gathering place for "stoners." They seemed to have perpetual open house and had every imaginable kind of game for people to play. Their friends and neighbors would come by; smoke pot and drink beer; and enjoy games together. P&A decided to start a Bible study amongst these people. Their visitors took to it amazingly well. Before starting this Bible study Pat had quit smoking pot. Since his little congregation had not yet done so, the question emerged as to whether or not he would allow them to smoke during the Bible study. We wrestled over this and prayed a lot. We wanted to avoid legalism. We knew the most important thing was that unbelievers were being reached and if their hearts were genuinely changed they would give up the weed. Finally the Holy Spirit impressed Pat and Alicia to ask their friends, out

135

of respect for them, not to smoke until after the Bible study. One by one their friends and neighbors came to faith in Christ and to a clean lifestyle. And some joined our church. P&A became key leaders in the life of our church especially in the crucial area of intercessory prayer and the midweek praise and healing service.[93]

---

[93] Pat and Alicia are still in touch with the people who came to their Bible study and for the last seventeen years have been strong servants of the Lord at the Dream Center (formerly Angeles Temple) in Los Angeles.

CHAPTER 22

Overflowing Life

By Christmas of 1986 Marilyn was able to stop her frequent visits to the doctor and lab tests showed she was in remission. She certainly looked much better and felt very good. We praised God at home and at church for His healing mercy. Meanwhile, we had started a midweek communion service at Silverlake. Initially, I had wanted a typical charismatic praise and prayer service, but the Holy Spirit kept whispering in my heart to make it a communion service and to have it at suppertime just as Jesus did when He met with His disciples at the Last Supper. We tried it during Lent and it went so well we just kept going with it. Initially my secretary, Mary, played the piano for our opening praise time. Soon we had an inspired little band that the Lord brought together made up of gifted young adults, some of whom were from Fuller. They were attractive and full of the joy of the Holy Spirit.

After the opening time of praise, we confessed our sins together, read a scripture, and after a prayer for illumination, invited whosoever to share what the passage said to them. People came prayed up and ready to share and it was a wonderful time of corporate ministry through the Word. Then everyone would circle the communion table and we would have one loaf of bread, fresh from the bakery. After blessing it and singing the Sanctus, we would pass it around and everyone would break off a piece. Then we would bless a chalice of unfermented wine, pass it around for them to dip the bread in and partake. As we passed the bread and cup from person to person, they would speak words of blessing to one another. After the communion, we would jointly pray for the concerns of the church family then break into small groups for the people present to pray unhurriedly for one another with the laying on of hands. Just before we took communion we would usually sing the Vineyard song by Michael Christ[94]:

> "It's Your blood that cleanses me,
> It's Your blood that gives me life,
> It's Your blood that took my place,
> In redeeming sacrifice,
> Washes me whiter than the snow, than the snow.
> My Jesus, Gods precious sacrifice."

It seemed as if in our practice, this song set the mood for the evening. There was a special anointing on the singing and the prayers that followed. Everyone commented on the sense of the presence of Christ. This service started with a few people in early '86, but quickly attracted numerous people. Usually we would have about fifty. There were many reports of

---

[94] Mercy/Vineyard Publishing

great blessing and healing. Periodically we would have special speakers who would inspire us, but mostly it was the priestly ministry of the lay people. It was the people's service where all the gifts of the Spirit came into play.

One night there were about eighty people present. After the communion several of our people said to me, "Did you see what happened?" And I said, *"What do you mean?"* To which some exclaimed, "You didn't notice?! There was more bread after the distribution than before." I was amazed. I said, *"Are you sure?"* (By that time the elements had been removed.) There were at least three people who said this to me. On another Wednesday night, the same thing happened, and again several people reported it to me. So I said to the Lord, *"Lord, what is going on?"* **"A whole lot more than you thought."**[95]

This confirmed to me, and to many others, that the Lord singularly blessed this midweek communion service. After reflecting on it a good bit, I changed my language concerning the distribution of the bread. I would say, *"Jesus is coming to us in and through the bread. He is coming to multiply His grace in you."* I believe when communion is faithfully done, it is not just a memorial service and it is more than a celebration of Christ's presence. He is coming to us and giving Himself to us. The fact that the gospels all tell us of the feeding of the 5,000, and two of them additionally of a

---

[95] Pat and Alicia were two of the people who witnessed this miracle. I did not make much of it for the reason that I was in touch with what was going on in San Antonio, Texas where Father Rick Thomas and his parishioners took food to the dump dwellers across the river in Juarez, Mexico and regularly saw the food multiplied when they didn't have sufficient to feed the poor.

feeding of 4,000 men, is food for thought. At first the disciples did not get the lesson of the multiplication. Later they did and it resulted in a high view of the Lord's Supper as seen in the Apostle Paul's writings.

CHAPTER 23

Sweet and Low

Marilyn, Sam and I loved it at Silverlake; we all felt accepted and cared for and supported in prayer. We had fun, too – we had monthly fellowship dinners and regular, well-attended, men's breakfasts. (Our cooks were superb.) These were times of relaxed and enjoyable interaction that enabled us to know one another. Some of our people put on plays and others put on art festivals, bazaars and musicals where many were able to develop their talents and bless the rest of us.[96]

Of course it wasn't all fun. We had our share of problems. It was a high crime area. There were a number of break-ins and vandalism at the church. Most of our Silverlake residents had their houses broken into at least once, many of our women had their purses snatched, and a number of cars were stolen during our services. Through prayer several cars were returned or retrieved!

---

[96] A number of our people were involved in the movie industry because Silverlake was formerly East Hollywood.

141

On February 7, 1987, we laid to rest beloved David duPlessis at Mountain View Cemetery, Pasadena, CA. I was honored and deeply moved to be one of seven chosen to speak at his funeral.[97] Since 1962 he had periodically checked in with me to counsel and pray. His influence was monumental.

In March '87 Amy called me. She was on break at the YMCA where she led aerobics classes. She was in tears. She said, "Dad, I just found out I'm pregnant with twins." I went right away. She had been so excited at her first pregnancy, but now the shock of discovering there were two babies made her fearful. It was a precious time to hear her spill out her fears and worries and to pray for her. It felt so good to convey the peace of God. In June two beautiful identical twins, Brendan and Connor, were born. Marilyn and I then had the joy of helping Amy and Mike with them and babysitting during the first three years until they moved to the Bay area in late '89. It was a crushing blow for me; it was hard to keep that special closeness since they moved five hours away.

In 1988 two of our Silverlake leaders complained to me about feeling oppressed by my anger and controlling spirit. Since Marilyn felt the same way, I knew I needed special help. Fortunately I knew a Spirit-filled psychiatrist and the Board of Pensions was willing to pay for therapy. I went to Dr. J for about a year. It was very helpful. He helped me face the fact that I was judgmental and my judging had brought a lot of hurt upon me. He had a vision of arrows sticking

---

[97] The others were Paul Schoch, Russell Spittler, Justus DuPlesses, and Fr. Killian McDonnell. G. Raymond Carlson, and David Hubbard.

in my back and we understood they represented the misfortunes I had reaped from my judging.[98] I saw that I was angry from what others had done to me and I needed to forgive at a deeper level. He also helped me see that my compulsive need to control others was based on a lack of trust in God and in others. It was wonderful to have a counselor who could not only help me face the truth but also pray for me at a deep level.

During my therapy I did the unthinkable. I faced my long repressed anger at my father. I had always worshiped him. My love and respect were strong. He tried to live the Sermon on the Mount; most of the time he was patient, kind and encouraging, but strict. I began to remember that when he decided I had done wrong (which was usually reported by my mother), he would not allow me to give my side of the story. Nor was I allowed to show anger towards him. No defense, no excuse was allowed. I was guilty as charged and spankings usually followed. This was particularly true during my fourth grade. I couldn't seem to spell accurately no matter how hard I tried. The spankings for poor grades, with an oak stick on my bare bottom, were devastating. Years later I learned I had a mild form of dyslexia. (I still can't spell.) By the release of the Spirit, I was able to forgive my father and find new freedom in forgiving others.

Another kind of therapy was that we rebuilt our kitchen and back part of our house, which was riddled with termites. Philip did most of the heavy work, and we had the fun of planning a new kitchen, bath and laundry. I did something I had always wanted to do.

---

[98] "Stop judging others, and you will not be judged." Matthew 7:1 NLT

I watched a professional tile setter for about a day, studied a booklet on tile setting, and then did all of the tile work for our new kitchen. For me there is enormous satisfaction in doing creative work with my hands. Actually, it is true for most everybody. That was also the case at Tahoe where I took classes in stained glass and produced two stained glass windows for our house. I would like to have gone on with the glass, but working with lead was bad for my lungs and I had to stop.

The church was growing. The contemporary service doubled the attendance. On October 31, 1988 our ushers reported to me that we had the largest Sunday attendance of my tenure at Silverlake. Then I remembered it was the anniversary of my trial before Phoenix Presbytery and I got choked up.

Marilyn had been keeping a record of all the happy times at Tahoe with our children, grandchildren and friends. Starting in late '89 she realized those happy times were coming to an end. She was finding it harder and harder to breathe at Tahoe (it was 6000' altitude). We could no longer ride our bikes together. In the early part of 1990 her ribcage was becoming painful. She dismissed it as arthritis but realized we needed to sell our Tahoe cabin. On her birthday, July 1st, we sold the cabin and invested in a rental property in Fresno.

I finally persuaded Marilyn to go to Dr. Elrod on August 7th. He sent her to St. Joseph's Hospital for tests on the 13th. She underwent a nuclear bone scan, chest xrays and mammogram. Two days later the oncologist confirmed Elrod's preliminary diagnosis. Her prior cancer had metastasized to her lower back, ribcage, neck area and skull. We met with the oncologist right away. I pressed him for a prognosis. At first he was vague – the usual talk about one never knows how long one has to live at any given moment. He finally admitted she had one to five years to live. He was hopeful that radiation would give her relief from the pain she was experiencing. Marilyn wrote in her diary, "Well – my reaction so far is that it hasn't really sunk in yet. I know the Lord will see me (us) through it. I can take comfort in the crucifixes on the walls at the hospital. Also – I never did want to be in an old folks' home. I do not want to be a burden – like be the center of attention of cleaning ladies, cooks, nurses, etc. – but how we'll manage financially is beyond me ... What about Bob? – I will take his time and thoughts too much so he can't be as effective as he needs to be in the church." The children were wonderfully supportive and caring.

The following Sunday I got very emotional and broke down in the pulpit. I told my people how bad it was and told them we needed their prayers more than ever; they were wonderful. There were lots of hugs and tears. Many people offered whatever to help Marilyn.

Marilyn hid her pain from me. I did not learn until 2014, when I found her diary, just how much pain she was in. She didn't want to divert my attention from my ministry concerns, but October 11, 1990, she wondered if she would last until her birthday, July 1, 1991. I did know she wanted to get out of the smog of Los Angeles. She wanted to be closer to Laura and Charlie and their children, Patrick and Shannon, our only granddaughter, in Santa Maria (on the Central Coast of California). Also to Phil and Anne and their boys Casey, Chad and Coby, in Arroyo Grande. Philip was building houses there and we had invested with him to build a spec house. On my days off I would take her to the ocean at Ventura. That was a blessing for her. I began to think about building a home for her in Arroyo Grande and to consider an early retirement. I talked to the doctors. I wanted their counsel. They confirmed my suspicions that it would be better to move sooner rather than later.

By mid-1991 I had come to a surprising conclusion. I not only needed to move for Marilyn's sake, but I needed to leave Silverlake Church for my own sake. The church had changed and grown wonderfully, but a new kind of leader was needed. I was weary with planning, programming with committees, hiring and supervising staff. I had been a pioneer in spiritual renewal; I was not an administrator. I loved preaching and teaching and loved to spend time with people and help them grow spiritually. I did not like running the organization. So, one by one I sat down with my leaders. I told them what my thoughts were and asked for their honest feedback. All but three told me reluctantly that it was time to go.

At first Joy and Jan were not accepting, but then Joy had a marvelous, moving sense of the presence of the Lord; she felt released from her fear of my going and felt a freedom to bless it. As I shared with Bill, he wept. Then he had a vision of me on a bike, riding free with the wind blowing through my hair and a sense that I no longer needed to pedal uphill.

However, there was some uphill pedaling before we could leave. We had to buy a piece of property in Arroyo Grande to build on and procure a bank loan to cover most of the land and building cost.

Also, our Glendale house needed to be prepared for sale. Unfortunately, we were in a mild depression and properties were not selling. Furthermore, we would need most of the proceeds from the sale of the Glendale house to pay off the bank loan by March or April. God's help was abundant. My daughter-in-law, Anne, found an ideal piece of property in the summer of '91, and we closed escrow in late September. We were able to get a loan and before long we got a reasonable offer on our Glendale house. In terms of presbytery procedures for my departure, we were able to make all the arrangements and I preached my final sermon on November 4th and the church had a wonderful farewell party for us. I told them and the Presbyterian Charismatic Fellowship that I would resume part-time my travelling ministry encouraging the renewal of the Holy Spirit.

Part of the week we would work getting our house ready for sale, part of the week I would travel to Arroyo Grande, and Philip and I began to plan the new house. By late November we were underway with the grading and with Philip and a partner working full time and myself part-time, we had the house ready for occupancy by my birthday, March 16, 1992. That was a very hectic day. It seemed like most of the church turned out to help us pack up 22 years of living with five children. A moving van took our big stuff and we rented a U-Haul truck and some of my men loaned pickups. The entire household was loaded up and moved in two days to Arroyo Grande. It was exhausting, especially for Marilyn, who was very much under the weather from cancer. But it was also great fun and fellowship.

CHAPTER 24

A New Place

I can't tell you how satisfying it is to build a new house and move into it and start life all over again in a new community. And Arroyo Grande is the best of places. It is on the Central Coast of California, a three-hour drive north of Los Angeles, and the climate is about as perfect as you would want. Most of the time the temperature is between 65* and 75* -- even in the winter when the temperatures can go down to the lower 40s, but by 9:30 in the morning it's warm and pleasant. It's a small town, and I'm a small town person. To get out of the smog of LA was wonderful. I remember Phil taking me out one night to our front yard and saying, "Look, dad, at the stars." They were spectacular. That's a rare discovery in LA. The icing on the cake is the beach is three miles away. When we moved here there were clams and sea otters that Marilyn delighted in.

The thing that energized me the most was finishing the house. The previous fall we had the joy of planning it and then once the work commenced in November, I divided my time between Glendale, getting ready to move, and Arroyo Grande working on the house together with Phil and his partner. It was fun staying overnights with my grandsons Casey, Chad and Coby. My work on the house was especially focused on the styling. I love Victorian architecture, so I had great fun in buying and applying all of the Victorian trim and paneling and selecting and painting the beautiful Victorian colors. This went on for a year or so after we moved in.

Also absorbing was our agricultural pursuit. We have a half-acre lot and went to work immediately to plant fruit trees for the future. Our favorites were two orange trees and a Meyer lemon. Eventually we had thirteen different fruit trees. We also planted vegetables and flowers. I was able to return to my teenage passion. Right away we got baby chicks and I obtained an old chicken house. Don't ask me what it is, baby chicks, clucking hens and colorful roosters are exciting to me. Before long we got ducks and put in a little pond and enjoyed them immensely. Then we got two sheep. I can still remember the lambs climbing up on my back while I leaned over to feed the chickens. They were such a joy. They are so silly and childlike. Both of them broke out of my poorly fenced yard. A neighbor helped capture one and tie him up, but the other made for the Village. Fortunately I was in good shape and pursued him through the Village, over the freeway, downtown, frantically trying to apprehend him before he caused an accident as he darted through traffic. It seemed like the whole community joined me in trying to catch him. A policewoman finally cornered him in a backyard a mile from our house. Several men put him in a pick up truck, tied him down, and drove him back home. I never worked so hard, so fast, to complete the fence.

I have to say there is something very special, maybe even mystical, about having animals around. This is part of why I always wanted to have a farm. There is a special communion that takes place between humans and animals and birds. I can't describe it. For me it's enormously fulfilling. I like to have them around. I even like to tease them a little bit. We had big dogs when we were in Glendale – that was good and it was special for the children, but somehow there was a more fulfilling level of life with sheep and later with a miniature donkey. To know sheep and donkeys first hand helps to savor and trust the Savior – they and He are the essence of meekness. The more I walk with Jesus, I know that's where I want to be.

I'm not only looking forward to heaven, but I'm also looking forward to that day when the whole creation will be renewed and the heavenly fellowship of people with Christ will be enriched with both domestic and wild animals living together in idyllic peace.

"The wolf shall dwell with the lamb, and the leopard shall lie down with the young goat, and the calf and the lion and the fattened calf together; and a little child shall lead them. The cow and the bear shall graze; their young shall lie down together; and the lion shall eat straw like the ox. The nursing child shall play over the hole of the cobra, and the weaned child shall put his hand in the adder's den. They shall not hurt or destroy in all My holy mountain; for the earth shall be full of the knowledge of the Lord as the waters cover the sea." Isaiah 11:6-9, ESV. (I literally believe this.)

Eventually we had our sheep sheared. That was fascinating. A professional shearer came and I couldn't get over how he would sit the sheep on her rump and turn her around while he cut the wool off with electric shears. The docility and cooperation of the animal was awesome. Then we washed the wool, had a person card it and spin it and Marilyn knitted it into an afghan for me. When it's chilly, there's nothing like a nap with that afghan covering me. It still has that special sheep smell.

The move to Arroyo Grande meant a new relationship with my church. I went from San Fernando Presbytery, which had not been very hospitable to my ministry, to Santa Barbara Presbytery where I found a ready welcome. There were churches that needed help. They had lost their ministers and before calling an interim they needed pastoral leadership. I was happy to help out and that opened doors for further opportunities to spread the renewal message. Also I found young ministers who were hungry for God and started coming to see me to be mentored.

Eventually I was able to help develop prayer groups and a yearly Presbytery conference on the Holy Spirit. At the same time I resumed working with the Presbyterian and Reformed Renewal Ministry (PRMI).[99] Working with Brad Long, we began to produce teaching manuals for leadership training. During the '90s I wrote one book-length manual on congregational renewal and collaborated on several others on prayer, healing, and the gifts of the Holy Spirit. In connection with that, we had some marvelous Spirit-filled conferences for the training of ministers and laymen at a beautiful

[99] Previously called Presbyterian Charismatic Communion

old hotel on the shore of Silver Bay, Lake George, New York and at a conference center called Bonclarken in North Carolina.

It was there in August, while I was teaching about prayer on a Saturday night, that a call came in from my oldest daughter, Emily. Her sister, Laura, had called her frantically. She and her family were vacationing in the mountains of Colorado and their three-year old little girl, Shannon, had fallen out of an attic window and had landed head first on granite rock. She was severely injured. She had landed in such a way that she was expected to lose the sight of one eye and there was fear she might lose her life from multiple skull fractures and blood clotting in her brain. Naturally, the atmosphere was such among the fifty plus attendees that the whole conference went to prayer for Shannon. I did not need to tell them, but they went on praying until about 1:00 AM and the conviction formed among us that she would be all right. I phoned Laura and told her *"Shannon will be all right. It will take awhile, but she will be all right."* As it turned out, they did not need to open her skull, the clots subsided, the eye mended without surgery and she fully recovered. She went on to become a young champion swimmer, a straight-A student and an attractive young woman who served as a Christian leader at college and went on to be a missionary for Campus Crusade for Christ.

The Shannon healing miracle, together with Sam's healing, became major sources of encouragement as I taught about prayer, healing and faith wherever I went. They also were sources of never-ending thanks and praise to our God of wonders.

Back in San Luis Obispo County, CA, I made a happy discovery. My old charismatic friend Abbot David Geraets had moved from his monastery in Santa Fe, New Mexico, to establish a new monastery on Cuesta Mountain. I began to attend early-morning prayer once a week with the monks and they welcomed me to their charismatic celebration of the Mass.[100] That commenced an enlightening seven year experience of learning Benedictine spirituality and being mentored by Abbot David. David taught me dream interpretation and encouraged me in contemplative prayer. We had sweet times of counsel and prayer. On the way home there was a wonderful place where I would have a sticky bun and a cup of coffee.

---

[100] The Mass is a worship service of scripture, praise, prayer and a celebrative recalling of the death of Christ for our redemption, and a partaking of His body and blood. When it is done in the Holy Spirit it is as good as worship gets.

CHAPTER 25

The Family

As we moved to Arroyo Grande I knew that time with Marilyn and the family had to be much more central. I had neglected her too much over the years, so I tried to make it up to her. Our family had always gathered together at Thanksgiving, Christmas, Mother's Day and her birthday, July 1st, and those times became more important than ever because we all knew time was running out. Our favorite routine was to gather in a beautiful outdoor place, be it the beach or a park or Lake Lopez and there we would not only barbecue and share potluck, but we would also play softball, volleyball or basketball. My children, and in the course of time, their spouses and children, were all excellent athletes. We would have terrific ball games and it was fun. The kidding and horseplay was sometimes hilarious. (In the early days, like when Charlie and Dale were at seminary and I was still youngish, inevitably Laura would say, "Let's get dad" and they would rush at me, get me down on the ground and wrestle with me as I had always done with them when they were little. Being roughed up and piled on was

154

truly gratifying!) It wasn't long before we could have two very good teams playing each other, especially softball. Marilyn enjoyed those times immensely, and it built strong unity in the family.

It was also my goal to try to take Marilyn to all the places she loved to go and new places she wanted to see. We were able to do a little bit of that our first year in the new house, but in '93, even though I had preaching missions twice a month, we managed to make five fulfilling trips. I'll mention two.

In September we revisited places in Alaska where I had preached, staying at the comfy townhouse of Ralph and Louise Weeks in Anchorage. We were awestruck by the beauty of Denali, inspired by the Iditarod dog teams and fell in love with the Puffins as we watched glaciers sheer off into the ocean. Most memorable was the raptor rehab center in Sitka where we saw wounded eagles being nursed back to health. We walked the short distance from our bed and breakfast very slowly and I ached for Marilyn. I knew she was hurting in her back and was pooped, but she wouldn't complain.

In October we flew back to southeastern Pennsylvania and soaked up our heritage amidst the beautiful fall foliage. We spent a day at Gettysburg and took it all in. I believe every American should go there and walk over the fields and hear the story. It's awesome. We researched Marilyn's roots in picturesque Lancaster. We learned why she never expected to live long; all of the women on her mother's side died young. She considered herself fortunate to have lived past 50 and she had no desire to be an old lady.

We visited my 93-year old father (who had been laid up for three years with strokes) and 89-year old mother in their retirement home. I surprised Marilyn and took her to her 45th high school reunion where she was deservingly the center of attention. Finally we relived the happiest days of her childhood by going back to her family cottage close to the ocean at Beach Haven Terrace, NJ. We ate superb seafood and roamed around her favorite sights.

Marilyn summed up the year by declaring, **"The steadfast love of the Lord never ceases, His mercies never come to an end; they are new every morning; -- the Lord is my portion, says my soul, therefore I will hope in Him."** Lamentations 3:23-24.

On January 24, 1994 (just shy of his 94th birthday), my father died at noontime on his mother's birthday. I had this delightful thought about it. *"How beautiful that he died just in time to have lunch with Granny in heaven."* I could just imagine them celebrating. (All his life he had gone up from the mill to his mother's house for lunch, along with some of his siblings and his father. Those were lovely times of stimulating conversation.) Most of my children and their spouses, together with Marilyn and I, went back to Philadelphia during a break in a huge snowstorm. We rented a big van together and had a great reunion with all of our eastern relatives, especially my sisters Joan and Martha and their families. It was a time of joy mixed with tears. The Memorial Service was held at my mother's church.[101] Mother's pastor did a beautiful job leading the service and I was privileged to preach. I

---

[101] This was the Sanctuary United Methodist Church, North Wales, PA, which was my mother's old family church where my great-grandfather Mahlon Moyer often preached as a lay preacher. I knew and loved him as a boy.

had prayed about it a lot. I had determined to identify with my father and his life and to tell his story as though it were my own. It was a high moment for me, and for the family. Laura said, "It was radiant, victorious, powerful, deeply touching and inspired." I have to say the dinner following the service was more like a wedding celebration. My most interesting conversation was with one of father's former Sunday school students. He told me that father rewarded him for being a very good student by taking him for a ride in his Jaguar sports car. (Father taught junior high boys until he was 88 years old and they never had an attendance problem.)

My first weekend back from Philadelphia, I did a preaching mission at a church in Camarillo, CA. I was still very tender and weepy. On Sunday night we had a healing service. A foster mother brought a three- month old baby girl. Her name was Tiffany. For six weeks she had been badly abused by her biological parents. She was emotionally distraught and her left eye had retinal damage and vision impairment (according to her doctor). When we prayed for her eye and her life, I felt such an unusual anointing as I touched her eyelid that I told her foster mother to have her checked again by the doctor. She did. The doctor found the eye perfectly okay, with no trace of damage or vision impairment, and the pastor subsequently reported that Tiffany became relaxed, cheerful and beautiful! I was deeply moved. The date of that healing was February 6th, my father's birthday. I felt in my spirit that a wave of healing power followed his death. I have talked to other healers and we agree; the strongest healings often follow a time of great difficulty and grief.

In early February '94, there was bad news and good news. Laura and Charlie were moving away from the Central Coast to LaJunta, Colorado and Emily and Dale were getting ready to move to Morro Bay, thirty minutes away from us. We had picked out a house for them. This was such a lift for us. We had been attending the local Nazarene church where Phil and Anne were leaders, but Marilyn felt more at home at Morro Bay Presbyterian and Dale became her pastor. It was so natural – we'd go to worship (when I was home) and then have dinner with Emily, Dale and the boys (Andrew, Daniel, Timothy). Then also I would preach for Dale when he was away, and helped in other ways with his church.

At home, Marilyn was well on her way to fulfilling a cherished goal; she wanted to knit a colorful, full-sized afghan for each of her ten grandchildren. Since she had to sit a lot and loved to knit, this was a pleasant way to wile away the hours, and I loved to watch the vibrant colors combine and emerge. Quite often I would be sitting nearby at a card table doing a jigsaw puzzle. Imagine the evening hours by the fireplace, with the needles softly clicking, the fire dying down, and the communion of silence. Few things are more satisfying.

By June '95 tests showed the cancer in Marilyn's back was on the march again. Through it all our daily prayers deepened. We lived more and more in the Psalms and we were comforted by great Christian music, times at the beach, visits of dear Christian friends like Joy Tinsley and Jan LaMoree from Silverlake, and by our children.

We discovered the cancer in her back had moved into her neck in late '96. In January '97 she had radiation every day in the neck area. It was effective for a while, but it left her with a dry mouth and difficulty in swallowing. It seemed she was living on ice cubes, cool drinks and applesauce. It was awful to see her suffer and she was worn out with the treatments. My hopes for a healing were fading away.

On Mother's Day we all gathered at Emily's in Los Osos;[102] we tried to make it a cheerful time, so of course we played softball. I got an infield hit – I tried to run like a young man to make it to first – all of a sudden I felt like I'd been shot in the right calf and hobbled to a bench. It was terribly painful. Later I learned from an orthopedist that I'd ruptured the calf muscle. I was crippled and had to go on crutches. I should have had surgery but I needed to take care of Marilyn every day. She needed more and more help around the house. She was becoming very tired. She was losing weight at a steady pace. It tore me up to see her going down.

Marilyn's selflessness and courage were terrific! One example tells it all. In late May of '97 her oncologist discovered golf ball size tumors in her right lung. Her first concern was for our youngest daughter Amy, on sabbatical in Spain until September. She didn't want to die in the middle of the summer and thus make it necessary for Amy to come home early. The doctor proposed there was one type of chemo that might get her through the summer alive, but it was likely to make her very sick. Even though she was worn out with radiation and toxic medicines, she immediately elected to take the "poison" so as not to spoil Amy's trip. I was sworn not to tell Amy and family how bad things were. Marilyn proceeded to take the medicine

---

[102] Los Osos is just south of Morro Bay

and keep taking it despite painful suffering. She held to her course until late August, when Amy returned. Then she went off medication so that she could enjoy (somewhat) her last two months visiting with her family. To the end her thoughts were all for others.

CHAPTER 26

Depths and Heights

The days dwindled down to a precious few. We could all see what was coming. The visits of children, grandchildren and friends became more and more unhurried and intimate. Beautiful expressions of love and caring became common. Marilyn was not afraid. She knew her life was in God's hands. She was cheerful and brave and delighted in her visits with people and in our heartfelt conversations with each other and with the Lord. One of her favorite things was for Philip to pick her up and take her for a ride on the beach. She loved to roll the windows down and inhale the wonderful salt air, especially since it was harder and harder to breathe. In early October her doctor, who was not at all given to dramatics, told her she had about a month to live. She quietly accepted this, because we knew it was the truth.

Family visits increased; Laura flew back from Colorado for a few days; Sam drove up from Glendale for some tearful times, and Amy came down from Moraga for helpful visits. Neighbors and friends started bringing food – I didn't have to cook much; we had plenty for family and visitors. For several weeks before she died, an unearthly quiet settled upon our house. We had stopped watching TV and were not even listening to Christian music. Friends, hospice nurses, food and floral deliveries, anxious phone inquiries, even the hissing and pumping of the oxygen machine could not make a dent on the silence and peace of eternity. It pervaded my soul like a healing balm while I watched my wife die. In the silence I could hear the still small voice of God speaking within more clearly than ever before. He beckoned me to go deeper into the silence with Him.

I had long wanted to go deeper with God. Marilyn was sleeping a lot and I was still hobbled by my calf. So I had plenty of time "to be still and know," to "wait on the Lord" to soak up His presence. I propped myself up on the bed in our guest room and started practicing again the prayer of quiet. In this kind of prayer we do not rush into the Lord's presence with our requests, but rather we seek to relax and wait expectantly for Him to speak while we concentrate on His great love and goodness revealed in Christ.

On Sunday night the 2nd of November, Dale and Emily and one of their elders from the Morro Bay church, together with their boys, came to lead us in a service of Holy Communion in our living room. It was a sacred time; though weak and unsteady Marilyn hung onto the memorable words of Christ to His disciples at the Last Supper knowing it was her last supper. After the service and many hugs and tears, she went to bed with her face set on dying as quickly as possible and going to be with the Lord. Though she continued on morphine for the pain, she asked to go off oxygen and for the next few days she took only a little water and a few spoonsful of custard and banana.

On Tuesday I wanted to call the nurse to give her a bath but decided, despite my disability, that I would do it myself. It was a very rewarding way of loving her and washing her tenderly. Emily came Wednesday (and Friday) and was a great help. For the next two days at times Marilyn was conscious, crying out to the Lord, at times she was out of it. I spent a fair amount of time, especially during the wee hours of the morning, lying next to her and praying. Friday morning the nurse told me she had no blood pressure, her heart was beating rapidly and she would die very soon. Phil thought he ought to stay the night with us. At 8:45 we laid down to sleep. At 10:00 we awoke to administer morphine. I realized she wasn't breathing. I checked her carefully. I told Phil, *"I think she's gone."* We knelt by the bed, we cried and we praised God that her suffering was over. We had great peace. The words came, **"Precious in the sight of the Lord is the death of His saints."** Psalm 116:15. It was Friday, November 7, 1997.

Phil said he felt her spirit go through the house about 9:00. He said it was like a gentle wind. The mortician came. After that the vacancy was like a vacuum. I felt it. The loneliness and yearning for her was overwhelming. I gushed tears. I phoned the children and they cried with me. Phil went home to bed. I slept fairly well and woke early. I praised the Lord for His goodness in taking Marilyn quickly; she was dying in earnest about five days – two of them were intense, labor – agony. The Lord gave me the hymn, "Near to the Heart of God."[103] I meditated on that hymn and enjoyed the communion with the Lord. He opened His heart to me. I praised Him for a beautiful day. There were lots of calls and visits. Tears were flowing, hugs abounded. Nevertheless, there was a pit in the midst of my abdomen that had started on Thursday. It was very painful at times but after a few days it went away.

Sunday was a glorious day. I made a big country breakfast, then went to the 9:00 service at Morro Bay and sat with Emily and the boys. I felt led to testify briefly about sorrowing with hope and how death has been abolished in Christ and life and immortality has come to light. Afterwards I went immediately to the 10:30 service at the Nazarene church and sat down front with Keith and Christa.[104] The church was packed. Pastor Ron was on a roll. He spotted me and invited me up to speak. I gave the same testimony. Then I was with Phil's family and later Amy and family arrived.

Monday morning I awoke at 2:30 with a song in the night. I spent an hour and a half meditating on Christ crucified – He was smiling (that was really new for me). I studied Psalms 63 and 42, both of which talk about praise and meditation in the night. Though my leg was as bad as ever, it was a wonderful morning because the fountain of the Holy Spirit was bubbling up within me as in the early days when the Holy Spirit first overflowed within.[105]

---

[103] Often in the morning a hymn or spiritual song comes to me. I receive it as a gift from the Lord and as His message to me for the day.

[104] Assistant Minister Keith Matthews and his wife Christa had been marvelously supportive to us through all of Marilyn's suffering.

[105] I was inspired to write Marilyn's obituary. See Appendix L.

That first week after Marilyn's death was typical of the nine months to come. There were many incoming and outgoing calls and in most of them I talked freely about Marilyn and what she had gone through and cried with my friends and relatives. It was also a time when I poured out my feelings to God, both of sorrow and of joy. Our bedroom had become a glorious chapel. I was having rich times of singing the hymns and songs of my faith and incredible times of feasting on the Word of God and communing with Him in spirit and in truth. Because of my loss it was the worst of times, but because of Him pouring His life into me, it was the greatest of times.

Amy stayed with me all that first week cooking and cleaning and helping to get ready for the Memorial Service, together with her siblings. Thursday Laura, Charlie and their children arrived from Colorado. Friday Mike and the twins returned. The Memorial Service was Saturday, November 15th at 1:00 at Morro Bay Presbyterian Church. I woke early for my usual time of praise and meditation and communion with the Lord. The first hymn that came to me was "Lift High the Cross." I sang it joyously several times and then "Majestic Sweetness Sits Enthroned." Then the Harter's arrived. They had come a long distance. Jeanne was Marilyn's closest friend in Chandler. They came into the bedroom for a wonderful visit while I propped up my leg. There were other wonderful visits and then Sam arrived in a suit! He drove me to the church. On the way I said, *"Lord, I sure hope You will show up."* He answered, **"Bob, you know I'll be there with great love."**

My kids and their families were all there in the narthex. They were greeting everybody with joyful love. The place was supercharged with love and the presence of the Lord. I was never more proud of my family. They had decorated the church beautifully with Marilyn's quilts in the narthex and on the communion table. The urn was on the communion table and behind it were beautiful red, white, blue and maroon flags and Marilyn's favorite protea flowers. With Dale leading, they conducted a service full of love and truth, a right balance of serious moments and humor. The opening hymn was Marilyn's favorite, "Beneath the Cross of Jesus." My sons-in-law are all good preachers and they were at their best. In addition, Philip and my oldest grandson Andrew spoke beautifully. God really showed up. I didn't need to say or do a thing. I was just awestruck and soooo satisfied. I didn't cry. I felt wonderfully lifted up. The congregational sharing time was super. Then we all went to the home of the Cone's on the shore of Morro Bay for a lovely reception that was more like a wedding feast than a funeral.

Afterwards as my family dispersed to their homes, though I knew times of terrible loneliness, it was mostly a time of getting back in touch with friends and relatives both near and far. I made up my mind I wanted to share Marilyn's story with people we hadn't been in touch with for years. In particular, I was able to get the phone numbers and addresses of people who were in our wedding party and old college friends and I had a ball rekindling our friendships. Also I went back to all the churches I had pastored and visited with my old parishioners. That was tremendously fulfilling. Particularly memorable was the trip I took with Emily to Tennessee. We had a marvelous visit for several days with the people of Allardt. It was so good to see what had become of all of them and to have rich fellowship. I also renewed my traveling ministry preaching and teaching in the churches that had long welcomed me. The most gratifying were the times I went back to Glendale. During the ten years of Darryl Johnson's ministry, the church had really blossomed in numbers and depth and life in the Holy Spirit. For a while I thought I might resume a position on staff. Nevertheless, I enjoyed encouraging the life of prayer and of the Spirit.

The hardest part of my grieving was periods of terrible guilt. I know there is no condemnation for those who are in Christ Jesus. However, I wrestled and prayed with self-condemnation over all the ways I had hurt Marilyn and disappointed her in the course of our long relationship. I especially deplored my angry outbursts and being critical and too controlling. Fortunately, I had wonderful friends who I could talk and pray with and they were an immense help. It is not enough to cry out to God, we need brothers and sisters who we can look in the eye and confess our shame and have them pray with us and assure us of God's forgiveness.

One of the strongest friendships during that time was with Dr. John DeVincenzo. While Marilyn was dying, his wife also was wrestling with terminal cancer. Through our mutual grief we formed a wonderful, close bond. At least once a week we would go to dinner together and talk things out. I do think we were like David and Jonathan. What a blessing!

167

God is so good. On February 18, 1998, he gave me a vision early in the morning. I saw two dogs; one looked like a Chow and the smaller one was carrying a red child's chair and I heard the words, "The big dog has a buddy." I had a good feeling about those dogs. I felt it was a message of hope and I suspected that the big dog represented me.

In September we (my children and grand-children) went back to Tahoe for a time of remembering Marilyn. We stayed in a house right near the one which we had built and had a marvelous time of motor boating, water skiing, and volleyball on the shores of Tahoma, Lake Tahoe. One morning we all went up in the woods where I had gone to pray in the past. There we had an intimate time of sharing, confessing our shortcomings and needs, recalling precious memories of Marilyn and praying for one another. It was a very healing time in her favorite place.

Soon thereafter I met an interesting woman (we'll call her Dee) and before long we felt we were very much in love. By December we got engaged and, of all things, we had my son-in-law Charlie commence marriage counseling with us.[106] We came from two different worlds. We clashed a lot. Unfortunately I was trying to shape her into the model Spirit-filled minister's wife and she was trying to get me to be relaxed, fun loving and minimally involved in ministry. I became aware, more than ever, of my defensiveness, self-righteousness, and controlling behavior. The engagement lasted a little over a month, probably because she was aware that

---

[106] Laura and Charlie had moved back from Colorado in the summer of '98 and he became Pastor of Templeton Presbyterian Church, forty minutes north of my home.

my love was not unconditional and she was tired of my trying to fix her.

By March '99 the tensions were such she commenced dating other men as well as me and I was feeling more and more rejected and unacceptable. I kept dating her because I loved her and believed in my heart she would eventually be a terrific sold-out-to-the-Lord person and we would make a great team. What I often feared finally happened. She terminated our dating because she was quite taken with another man. I was crushed but I had learned valuable lessons that would make me a better and more marriageable person.

In August I was hurting and grieving so much that I called together some of my intercessors and my dear friends, Kirk and Denise Schauer to pray for me. Without giving them any details of what I was going through, I asked them to pray for a word from the Lord for me. After awhile Kirk said, "At your feet I see a pile of broken glass of different colors." I said, *"That pretty well describes how I feel."* Then he said, "Wait, it's not broken glass, they are pieces of cut glass. They are blue, white and pale rose." Then he said, "I see them coming together in a beautiful stained glass window." I felt wonderfully comforted. There were other words too. One of the women saw me being married but couldn't see who the woman was but said it would happen soon.

Dear John arranged a get-acquainted meeting for me with a younger Christian woman, Carolyn, from Cambria on August 19th. I got to Hoppe's Bistro in Morro Bay first. I stood in a vacant parking spot to save it for her arrival. In a few minutes she drove in and saw me standing there. As she looked at me she felt the warmth of the Holy Spirit go from the top of her head down through her body and heard the words, **"That's the man you're going to marry."**[107] Understandably she was staggered by this news. She was not looking for a husband because she was recently widowed. As she emerged from the car I wondered what ailed her, she appeared to be preoccupied (I hesitate to say "drunk"). We exchanged greetings and went in to have the most delightful laughter-filled conversation I'd had in a long time. I was totally myself. I even asked her to split a dinner with me and as usual, too cheap to buy an expensive dessert, I took her to Foster's Freeze where our conversation deepened and ended in prayer. The next day I told many of my family and John I had made a wonderful new friend. She went home and told her best friend she had met a minister she was going to marry. For the next few weeks we would meet again on the same night of the week (when we had originally intended to go to a grief group). So we jokingly called our dates, "grief group."

---

[107] Wisely she did not share this astounding news with me for a few weeks.

CHAPTER 27

An Open Heart

From the start Carolyn and I shared our stories. We seemed to tell each other everything. In about two weeks she told me how the Lord told her I would be her husband. Since she was only sixteen months old in the Lord, I reminded her that all revelations need to be tested by scripture, prayer and mature counsel. (Privately, I mostly believed her.) I also told her all about Dee and how I was still in love with her and was still grieving her rejection and my loss of her and Marilyn. I told her these things with tears. When I was finished she grabbed me and hugged me. It was an unforgettable moment of empathetic love.

Carolyn amazed me. She was more hungry and receptive spiritually than anyone I have ever known. From the start she wanted to know everything I knew about God and wanted to receive all His goodness. The Saturday following our first meeting she showed up at my training class at the Nazarene church for prayer servants. And the next day she came to the early service I was preaching at Dale's church in Morro Bay. It was that way every week.

Right away Carolyn wanted the fullness of the Holy Spirit. She had been prepared because she had joined a little Pentecostal church in Cambria and was already leading the prayer group. Quickly she experienced the Holy Spirit's power and gifts. She had been through a lot of hurt including sexual molestation as a child and abusive relationships with men. She wanted me to pray for the healing of her memories and many of our dates were spent in such prayer. It was always rewarding to pray for her because she experienced the Lord's grace demonstratively. Several times in the first few months of our praying and worshiping together, she saw Jesus coming to her, speaking to her and imparting His love and joy. These visions were unique and humbling. Jesus wore a brown rustic robe; his bare feet were dirty, when He came close to touch her she could smell His sweat and blood, and see His matted hair. She would be reduced to weeping and praying heartfelt prayers of repentance and adoration. The spillover on me was deeply moving and healing. I thought to myself, *"I never was comfortable with the classic pictures of Jesus in white robe, beautiful face, carefully combed hair and halo, but this was the real suffering and sacrificing Jesus."*

The thing that impressed me most was that Carolyn was so gutsy and compassionate. One story stood out. Her brother-in-law, Kenny, was gay and had AIDS. In the last stages of his illness, with no insurance and no one to care for him, Carolyn took him into her home. He was in great pain and developed horrible sores and wasted away. Day and night she bathed and massaged him and expressed her love for the last three months of his life.

Another thing that struck me about her was Carolyn was uniquely gifted in terms of her spiritual revelations. Often she would get the word of knowledge,[108] discerning of spirits,[109] and she had a strong healing gift. When she would lay hands on people to pray for their healing, they would feel a lot of heat coming through. She also had a strong ability to empathize and cry with the hurting. In addition, she was unafraid to speak out anywhere for Jesus and to confront when necessary.

I often reflected why Carolyn was so gifted. The more I knew her and the more I prayed for inner healing, the more I realized she had suffered a lot in terms of molestation, obesity, kidney disease and heart disease and it had prepared her to be a pure channel of God's redemptive grace.[110]

Trips to and from Cambria increased; our relationship ripened fast. My children began to get acquainted with her. Friends were telling us they could see we were meant for each other. In so many fundamental ways we were alike. Once, we were in a furniture store and she saw a small child's chair and exclaimed how she loved little chairs. It stopped me in my tracks. I remembered the vision of the big dog with his smaller buddy with the little child's chair.[111] I knew

---

[108] The word of knowledge is an inner knowing of what is going on, as when Jesus knew what the Pharisees were thinking about him.
[109] Discerning of Spirits is awareness of the presence of demonic spirits.
[110] After suffering for years with Polycystic Kidney Disease and dialysis she lost both kidneys in 1997 and later that year received a transplant. Soon thereafter she had open-heart surgery to replace her aortic valve. During all of that she was caring for her obese husband who was disabled due to multiple strokes.
[111] See page 168

that Carolyn was my buddy, that we saw things alike and in basic ways we were like Chow dogs.

There were some tensions. My grief was healing slowly and Carolyn was in a hurry to get married. She would say, "What's your problem? The Lord told me you were going to be my husband." Then I got sick with the flu. Keep in mind she was living with a transplanted kidney, which means she was on immune suppressant drugs that made her very susceptible to disease. Nevertheless, she wanted to take care of me; I could hardly do anything for myself. For a couple of days she traveled from her house to mine (a two hour round trip). Then I told her she might as well stay in my guest room. Her Florence Nightingale behavior (and her chicken soup) sold me. She even drove me to the jeweler to get her engagement ring. We asked Keith to do a quick job of marriage counseling. He gave us all the profile tests and said we were the most perfectly matched couple he had ever seen.

I contacted my children to see when would be a good time for a wedding. They were troubled. They felt it was too soon and that we hardly knew each other. They were dragging their feet in terms of agreeing on a date. All along I had been talking to my mother. She had been a wonderful comfort through all of my grief and when I told her the situation, she said, "Bobby, they will never accept it until you do it. Go ahead and get married." So Saturday afternoon, January 15, 2000, my bride and I walked down the aisle of the Nazarene church to meet with Keith and Christa standing behind a communion table. Carolyn was gorgeous in a silvery grey silk suit and blonde hair and blue eyes. Keith conducted a moving marriage service culminating in the four of us taking communion together. Then I looked up and saw the old stained glass windows, blue, white and rose[112] and felt like falling on my face in praise to God for His marvelous design and mercy.

---

[112] See Kirk's prophecy on page 169 to understand why I was so overcome.

CHAPTER 28

Worship

As we began a new life together, worship was central. Our usual custom was to go to the Nazarene church. But there were difficulties. The Holy Spirit was working so powerfully in Carolyn that the physical manifestations were rather demonstrative. The raising of hands[113] and swaying to the music was customary at New Life Nazarene. But Carolyn wanted to dance in the aisle and when Jesus was named she would crunch.[114] If the message were really anointed she would go face down on the floor[115]; at times her arms would gyrate so that some wondered if she had Tourette's syndrome. She

---

[113] The raising of hands in worship was the traditional posture of Hebrew and Christian prayer right up through the Reformation (see Psalms 63:4, 134:2 and 143:6). It symbolizes surrendering to God, offering ourself to Him, and delighting in His victorious presence.

[114] Crunching is a quick, spontaneous bowing at the waist compelled by the Holy Spirit. (Psalm 95:6)

[115] In scripture priests, prophets and presbyters fall down when God manifests His presence (1 Kings 8:1-11. Daniel 10:8-9, Acts 9:3-4, Revelation 4:10).

cried and laughed a lot.[116] I loved to watch her worship because she worshiped with her whole body and mind and voice but, to put it mildly, it was distracting to other people.

I thought to myself, *"This will never go at Presbyterian churches when I do a preaching mission."* When I did go, I would have her sit in the back or in a corner hoping no one would see her. There were a few places where we got away with it. What to do?[117]

I resolved I would not put a lid on Carolyn's spirit. I knew that everything she was doing was well known among the ancient Hebrews and among the Pentecostals. I decided that if her behavior closed the doors to my Presbyterian mission, so be it. I would find a place where she could worship the Lord with all her heart and soul and body. This was not an easy resolution. My whole mission had been to bring the message of the Holy Spirit to the Presbyterians. Through our friends Kirk and Denise we found a haven at the Santa Maria Vineyard Church.[118] In conformity with blessed John Wimber, the Santa Maria church was wide open to all of the workings and manifestations of the Holy Spirit. I had the joy of watching Carolyn week by week pour out in unrestrained adoration what God was so richly pouring in all through the week. I loved the way at the mention of Jesus' name she would bow

---

[116] Biblical worship was exuberant and demonstrative (see 1 Chronicles 15, Psalms 47:1, 66:1, 98:4-6, and 150:3-5, Lamentations 2:18-18, Hebrews 5:7).

[117] One time Carolyn went down on the floor between the pews and wanted to crawl into the aisle for more space to manifest and I blocked her, all the while hoping no one noticed.

[118] Meanwhile, I continue to be a member of the Presbytery of Santa Barbara.

down. She could not restrain herself from doing that. I realized the Holy Spirit causing her to do this had to be the origin of Catholic genuflection.

During the week in our home we made it our practice to worship God every day together. We would read and discuss the scriptures systematically. We would praise the Lord in song and prayer and we would pray for the many intercessory concerns that God laid on our hearts. Early on I was astonished one morning when the power of the Holy Spirit came upon Carolyn and she started to laugh hilariously. She laughed so hard she doubled over, fell out of her chair and rolled on the floor with incredible laughter and joy. I loved it. It refreshed me. She was like a child rolling in the snow and I was wishing I were free enough to do it with her. I have told her many times that I thought she was an attractive person, but when she's a holy roller she's absolutely beautiful and delightful.

At nighttime we began from the start to practice mutual confession and forgiveness. She instigated it. She would say, "Have I said or done anything to offend you or hurt you today? If so, please tell me so I can ask your forgiveness and repent." Then she encouraged me to do the same with her.[119] Then we would ask God to forgive us and give us grace to truly forgive one another from the heart. What this meant was that hurts, misunderstandings and resentments were not allowed to build up. Over the years we have practiced this, not as rigorously as at first, but regularly, and it has kept our marriage love fresh. The essence of our Christian faith is to walk in humility. Without confession to God and to one another pride works insidiously and takes

---

[119] Our guide in this practice is Ephesians 4:25-31.

a terrible toll of our relationships. So we plead with all of our friends and family to confess their sins to one another in the presence of God and be healed. (Please see James 5:13-20.)

Both at nighttime and in the morning we intercede for loved ones, people we are ministering to and for various causes, and once again Carolyn taught me a lot about prayer. In certain incidences the Spirit would come upon her and she would groan and cry when she prayed for the needs of others.[120] At times she would pray so passionately that her whole body would wrestle and contort like one who is in combat and agony. I came to see that Biblical prayer is not sedate or detached but passionate and more a cry of the heart than a carefully worded petition.

It's important that I share about my own times of private prayer that I usually do early in the morning. My best times of prayer have been when I practice contemplation, or the prayer of quiet. I enter into prayer with praise, then read and meditate on some scripture (usually a short passage). Here is an entry from my journal of June 2000. *"I meditated on Philippians 3. I chose to concentrate focusing on Jesus within. I asked Him to take me in deep – I prayed the longings of my heart to come into the secret place of the Most High. Came into a profound contemplative state – sought to observe carefully what it is: profound and pervasive silence; wonderful peace, a sense of serene security; a sense of spaciousness within a sphere of security;*

---

[120] Luke 22:44, Colossians 1:29, 4:12, Romans 8:26, 15:30. The word Luke uses for Jesus praying in the Garden is the Greek "agonia" and the word Paul uses in Colossians is the Greek "agonizomai." In Galatians 4:19 and 4:27 Paul uses the word for a woman travailing in birth to describe his prayers for the troubled Galatians.

awesome quiet, stillness and rest despite household sounds of heater, clock and neighborhood sounds; wonderful collectedness in the inner sanctum of His presence. I quietly praised the Trinity. Didn't want to come out, but it was time. I saw a hornet drowning in a glass of water. So – the prickly, stinging part of me (that gets upset and angry) is being drowned in the Living Water."

CHAPTER 29

Liberating the Oppressed

I suppose we broke all the rules. Our first year together was not only a honeymoon and a time of adjustment to each other's way of living, but I was intensively praying for the healing of Carolyn's deep hurts, especially childhood sexual molestation. Before long she also began to pray for my hurts. One might think being lovers and also doing spiritual therapy on one another would not be good, but actually it kept bringing us to a deeper understanding of one another and a greater appreciation of what we had been through and the lessons we had learned.

Within a few months we discovered people who desperately needed inner healing and started on a regular basis to meet with people, hear their stories and pray for them in our home. The interesting thing was we seemed to attract people who had been through the same hurtful things we had been through ourselves. We were truly able to empathize with them and many of them found some degree of healing. Some of these people experienced enough healing they were able to pray effectively for others.

Within a year we began holding inner healing meetings at our church in Santa Maria every other Sunday night. At first there were only a small cluster of people who came; people we had already prayed for. Then others began to trickle in until there were normally 35 or so people. Initially we would break into small clusters to pray for one another and the leaders were those who had become more experienced. Eventually God led us to do something daring. We would ask for volunteers to come up front and share their stories of hurt in front of the whole group. We would then dialogue with them and pray for them as a demonstration to all present about how to pray for such things as molestation, rape, abandonment, rejection, alcoholic parents, childhood physical and emotional abuse, etc. It was astounding how people opened up with their most intimate hurts and always God showed His healing presence. Naturally some people needed extensive ministry over a period of time. These would end up in our living room one by one over a period of weeks or months. Some we prayed for more than a year.

Polly is a good example of the kind of person we prayed for long-term. She never felt loved as a child. Her parents never told her they loved her and their approval was always conditional. Because she was not able to excel in the things that were important to them, such as good grades, music and ballet, she was treated as unacceptable and punished for not meeting their expectations.

Her parents were abusive and mean. Her father was controlling and severe. Even her mother was afraid of him. She was spanked daily with a black strap when her dad came home from work because she was always in trouble for something. She would cower in a corner, waiting in fear, until he came home, knowing she would be whipped. Polly was not allowed to have feelings or an opinion. "We were never allowed to speak, because the only opinion that mattered was dad's. We were never asked how we felt about something or what we liked. It was, 'Take what you get and don't complain or ask questions; just do what you are told and keep your mouth shut.'"

Polly's low self esteem made her an easy target for being dominated and mistreated. She didn't know who she was or what she liked or what she should expect from other people. "It seemed completely normal and right to me that my feelings counted for nothing; I would do and say, and go along with, whatever the person said or did." She felt she deserved to be mistreated by men. "I had to submit and try to please, because if I did not, they would get angry and abusive." Polly lived in a fantasy in her mind for years, blotting out the ugliness of the past, thinking it was okay and going from one dysfunctional relationship to the next. She was divorced from the father of her first two children and was living with an ungodly man who fathered her third child. He did not want the responsibility of a family. She felt alone and desperate. She turned to God and promised Him she would do whatever He told her if she could just have a better life. She realized she needed help with her parents and her ex.

We taught Polly that above all she needed to deal with the deep hurts from her father and mother, which she had buried. Week by week we prayed for her to remember and relive the most important painful memories of her childhood and to realize scene by scene that Jesus was there with her, hurting with her and loving her. Most importantly we helped her release her anger and judgments to the Lord and to forgive specifically the things that had been done. We also helped her learn as much as she could about her parents' backgrounds so she could understand them better. Her father was an orphan and had been raised in a terrible situation where he had been brutalized. After about a year of remembering and forgiving, Polly went from being emotionally dead – unable to feel or cry – to being free and in touch through the love of Jesus. Her children have grown up, are happily married and doing well. She, herself, has married again to a humble and faithful Christian man. She is one of the most joyous people we know.

Another example of our ministry is Rex. His in-laws asked us if we would be willing to see him for the sake of their daughter. We told them we were already overloaded but we would pray about it. That night I had a dream in which I saw a gun that was locked up and I had the key to unlock it. The next morning I knew I had the key to unlock Rex. I discovered he had been immersed in pornography since he was a teenager. He had learned it from his father who kept a stack of pornographic magazines in their bathroom. Even after he accepted Christ as his Lord and Savior at the age of twelve, he was addicted to pornography.

As I began to pray for Rex I asked the Lord to bring to his mind the key memories of his childhood he needed to deal with. He remembered first of all his mother who had been divorced from his father. She had always worked. She had never been there when he came home from school and he resented her for being absent, messy and passive-aggressive. She continued to be a problem in his marriage. I prayed God would help him see his mother as He sees her. He saw his mother as a small child riding a broken tricycle, one of the rear wheels was badly broken, yet she rode on and dragged it along with her. He saw her as a plucky survivor who had always done the best she could with what she had. He began to forgive her and love her.

Rex came to see me as a very angry and impatient person. As I dealt with memories of his father he saw clearly he learned impatience from his father yelling at his wife who always seemed to frustrate him. Jesus gave him new insights about his father and his weaknesses and he began to forgive him deeply in his heart. He also began to realize that too often he treated his wife the way his father had treated his mother and he began to repent. In time he saw that while his father had corrupted him, he had corrupted his brother and realized he needed to ask forgiveness of his brother and did so.

As I continued to meet and pray Rex realized he was spending too much time with worldly friends telling crude jokes. He realized he had to separate from them and cultivate Christian relationships. He began to see he had a critical spirit toward the church and he was too critical at home. We prayed through the things that had happened and he forgave those involved, and cultivated patient love.

As with all of our counselees, we would pray daily for Rex and his relationships so we were surprised when after seven months he confessed he had slipped back into pornography. He repented and committed himself to scripture meditation using his imagination as in the case of Tom on pages 131-133. As I prayed for him to be restored to purity, he saw Jesus come with fiery hands and embrace Him in purging fire. He also began to learn to cultivate a biblical self-image and to forgive himself for his short-comings. We've had the privilege of watching Rex grow along with his lovely family for ten years. He is one of God's gifted ministers.

The following are some snapshots from our inner healing ministry:

As we prayed about Dino's mother, he began to cry and wail (I worried about what the neighbors were thinking). It was the most pitiful expression of pain I'd ever heard. He felt she was unable to affirm him or express affection; she was addicted to criticizing and rejecting. He cried half an hour. Then as we prayed for Jesus to reveal truth, he saw a hole in her heart and then a hole in her mother's heart and it came to him that she had nothing to give and he began to forgive her and love her anyhow.

Lou remembered when he was six and got in trouble. His mom told him in anger she was sorry he was ever born and cussed him out. Then she said she would love him less and less if this continued until finally she would do to him what she had done to his dad, whom she had divorced. As we prayed he saw in his mind Jesus coming to him embracing him and telling him he was a pearl of great worth.

One of the first times we prayed for Nancy, as we asked the Lord to come to her, she saw an Easter basket full of colored eggs. They represented things the Lord wanted to deal with in her life. She chose the purple one. As she did so she had a vision of her dad trying to suffocate her as a baby. As we prayed for her to be in touch with her feelings, she really began to feel enormous anger. So much so, she screamed in a primal way. Then she asked Jesus to take that anger and help her to forgive her dad. She also renounced a vow to be quiet and unobtrusive and as small as possible. Each time we met for prayer she would choose another colored egg to open. They truly were resurrection eggs because each time she faced the terrible abuse she went through, she experienced the healing presence of the Risen Christ.

Wilfred was a ticking time bomb. It didn't take much to make him explode. His first memory was when as a small child he was stung by a jellyfish. He came out of the ocean screaming and crying. His dad beat him to make him stop crying. That became the usual thing. As an altar boy he was abused by a drunken priest and then forbidden to be an altar boy. He felt he had an angry demon. As he relived and forgave incidences of awful treatment we cast out a spirit of anger in Jesus' name.

We will always remember Sparky. She relived as though in a dream her father molesting her as a small child. I can still see her desperately pulling down her dress and pleading, "No, daddy, no daddy, it hurts." The scars of her molestation were typical of the many we have prayed for. She became obese. She's always had difficulty sleeping. She had suffered from life-long depression and an eating disorder. She went through five marriages. She battled to regain self-esteem.[121] It took a few years to work through her traumas with Jesus. She was diligent. Gradually she was healed.

---

[121] See Appendix M, "Signs of Sexual Molestation"

For a number of years now she has been praying with others for their healing.

Then there was Nel. She was heavily involved in the occult --- went to channelers and received a spirit guide named Bobagee. She was in a horrible accident and unconscious for three days; she felt she was in a cold, dark place. But Bobagee came to her, incorporated her body into his and "protected her" from the cold and (she felt) enabled her to survive. He also persuaded her she had lived in a previous incarnation. We had her relive her times with Bobagee and asked Jesus to reveal the truth. She was astonished to see her nice little friend was a deceiving spirit. She renounced him in the Name of Jesus and also all her involvement in the occult. She asked forgiveness of the Lord and we prayed for her to be set free in the Holy Spirit. She felt like a windstorm blew through her and made her clean.

CHAPTER 30

The Blessing of Repentance

My favorite time of year is autumn. Then the best place to be is northeastern United States. We went back in late August 2004 to visit my mother. She was dying. We spent some lovely days reading the Gospel of Mark to her and seeing her get all excited about it. Her countenance was glowing. She couldn't get enough of it. We had some wonderful talks. Our relationship had been good for a long time. She died September 30th shortly after we had to come home. She just missed her 100th birthday January 19th. My memories of her are sweet. All was forgiven and understood.

It was a productive time. The first five years of the new century I dictated and Carolyn typed and produced numerous teaching pamphlets to encourage people we were praying for.[122] All of the praying and producing made me willing to do what I had always said I wouldn't do. Carolyn took me to Hawaii for our fifth anniversary! (It was the first of three relaxing and joyful visits to the islands). I can never forget the balmy

---

[122] See my blog www.BobsGodBlog.blogspot.com for the written material.

breezes and the beautiful shores of Kona. We'd wake up every morning to a chorus of hundreds of birds in a huge tree just outside our window and at night we'd hear them again in one last hurrah before they slept. They are our teachers: to praise God first thing in the day and the last thing at night.

I've mentioned that Carolyn and I prayed a lot for each other. She was facing her sins and repenting and I was doing the same. One thing kept humbling me and baffling me. I was crippled. Since my calf injury in '97 I had never fully recovered. Despite physical therapy and constant exercises, soaking and stretching, my right leg would not work right. If I walked much or worked too hard in the yard it was painful and frustrating. I felt as if there was something in the calf that was tearing if I walked normally so I had to walk with small steps sort of duck fashion. Sometimes it was so bad I'd be on crutches or a cane. 2004 was a turning point. It was more and more clear my leg would worsen under stress, but especially when I was angry and judgmental. While praying for me Carolyn had a vision of a Dutch door. She said to me, "You're not open to your children like you are to God; when they hurt you, you withdraw and shut the door." I realized, *"I have to stay open with them and I have to continually repent of critical and judgmental attitudes."*

But there was more than my attitude. One day in prayer Carolyn saw a bull's eye. We felt it was a demon and did spiritual warfare. I asked, *"Why are you attacking me?"* The demon answered, "Because I don't like you." Two days later in prayer, Nancy discerned a little sharp-toothed critter attacking my leg. (Just the day before I dreamt of a rat attacking my leg.) The demon was on a leash attached to a big demon above. We (Nancy, Mary, Carolyn and I) came to the conclusion the big demon was anger which had come down through the Whitaker line. (There was also plenty of anger coming down through my mother's family.) I confessed and renounced a recent angry outburst at a young man, who was giving me a hard time during a preaching mission, forgave him and committed myself to apologize to him. As I did so, Nancy saw the big demon shrinking down to a small size. Then she saw it becoming a puddle as I repented for the sin of anger of my ancestors. The next day my leg was substantially better. I was able to do toe lifts with no stabbing twinges or tearing sensations.

All was well until late July. We were going to the beach and were judging an obese woman whom we had counseled the day before. I got a series of sharp pains in my calf until I repented. So I said to myself, *"It is not only anger, but judgment."* For a week I came against anger and judgment. I renounced them. I bound them in the Name of Jesus. I cast them out in the Name of Jesus. And I trusted anew that through the blood of Christ I am dead to sin. My leg got very well despite a strenuous project in the yard.

But I was not out of the woods yet. I had to go on crutches to the local car show with my son. So we met with my buddies again. They did soaking prayers on my calf and in a vision saw Jesus do surgery on it and cut some little knot out of it with His sword. Afterwards my leg was better than it had been in five months. But there was a second soaking/surgery on my calf a week later. Our friends discerned we were prompting each other to peevishness, irritation and criticism. We repented. The rest of the year my leg was perfect and I could walk anywhere, even on uneven ground, without any problems. I'm so glad for what I had learned before my last days with my mother.

BUT .... During our vacation in Hawaii in January '05, after a walk through the rainforest, for the second time in a week Carolyn dropped our new camera on the road. She interpreted my upset look as, *"You're stupid."* Actually I was judging and condemning her. She reacted by throwing the camera into the backseat of the car. Then I was really condemning. For two days my miserable leg was difficult to walk on until I forgave her in my heart and two days later asked her to forgive me for condemning her. Then my leg rapidly healed and it was happy Bobby and Carolyn once again.

This painful story is illustrative of what we have learned over and over again in our own experience and the lives of our many counselees. There is an intimate connection between our physical wellbeing and our spiritual condition or mental attitude. We found the most crippling sins are unforgiveness and judgment in our hearts. We have found the key to joy and peace is to be quick to face these rotten attitudes and repent of them. We are not saying all adverse physical conditions are due to our own sin; we cannot make that judgment. But we are saying many of our medical conditions can get amazingly better or totally healed with ongoing ruthless honesty and repentance.

We have learned when we have back pains to say, *"Who is on my back?"* or *"Who is a pain in my rump?"* Amazingly a face or name comes to mind and we realize there has been mounting irritation with that person and we must forgive and stop judging them. When we have a stiff neck we have learned to say, *"Who is a pain in the neck, or whom am I rebelling against?"*

CHAPTER 31

Patient Endurance

One of the most important things my father taught me was about patience. He would see how frustrated I would get with the normal trials and setbacks of life. Then he would say, "Just remember young man, we are in the school of life. God is teaching us many lessons. The most important lesson is to learn to patiently endure. We are in a great gymnasium. As we learn the simpler lessons, like jumping off a trampoline, we progress to the harder lessons of balancing on the horse. Eventually we progress to the rings. When we have learned all of the lessons here below, we graduate to the great university above." Then he would say, "You have to take the trials of life in stride and without complaining." What he didn't say (but firmly believed) is that in the great chapter on love in 1 Corinthians 13:4-7, the quality of love which is most emphasized by Paul is patience. **"Love is patient ... love does not insist on its own way; it is not irritable ... love bears all things ... endures all things."**

I thought surely by the age of 75, and considering all I'd been through, I'd learned patient endurance. How wrong I was.

In the spring of 2005, Carolyn became very sick. On the mirror in my bathroom is a list of all the symptoms I must be aware of when she is sick. When I went over the list, I realized it was time to go to the hospital. She was undergoing renal failure; her transplanted kidney was on the skids. Fortunately Dr. Wolfe was very alert and with his immense experience was able to prevent the loss of her kidney. However, it was badly damaged and she began a course of greatly reduced energy and frequent pain and discomfort. Naturally we quickly went through the process of getting on the list for a new kidney transplant. We chose to be listed with the University of California San Francisco Transplant Center. The woman who signed us up assured us that within a year we would probably receive a new kidney.

How little she knew. There was a long wait and during that wait Carolyn became increasingly sick due to toxins building up in her system. Increasingly she was unable to help with the teaching of our Sunday night group at Santa Maria. We needed to save energy. By '06 we realized it was foolish to drive twenty minutes to church in Santa Maria when there was a good Vineyard right here in Arroyo Grande. We turned over the leadership of our inner healing ministry to Nancy and teammates and started anew at Five Cities Vineyard. There we resumed counseling and praying with people for inner healing and other needs, but in Carolyn's case she could not do as much.

By 2009 the one-year wait for a new kidney had become four years and Carolyn was increasingly sick and weary. Her doctor decided she would have to be prepared to go back on dialysis (which she had gone through before her first kidney transplant.) This meant surgery on her upper right arm to fashion a fistula (portal) where the hemodialysis needle would be inserted. After a painful recovery it was obvious the surgery needed to be improved upon and so a second surgery was performed and it also was not right. So a third surgery had to be performed and to our dismay it was not adequate either. After several consultations it was decided that what she had always dreaded would have to be done. She would have to have a shunt put in her abdominal wall for peritoneal dialysis. This operation was successful and after six weeks or so she was ready to start dialysis again.

I have to say through all the surgeries and the waiting times between them, I was at the end of my rope. I could see my wife wasting away; she looked like skin and bones and I could tell she was sicker and sicker. Nothing seemed to be working right. I was seeing a repeat of what Marilyn had gone through and I was scared. I wondered why all of our prayers for successful surgery were not being answered. I feared she would die before she would get a new kidney. There was a battle to maintain a hopeful and positive spirit and to believe that somehow she would survive. Unfortunately my strong gift of empathy became my enemy. I agonized over everything she was going through.

The plan was for Carolyn to administer peritoneal dialysis to herself at home. She would do it four times a day about an hour each time. Our hallway and garage were lined with boxes of dialisate fluid. Carolyn was taught how to administer it to herself and things did not go well. There were endless problems and more suffering for her. I was hanging on to the words of James 1:4, **"Let patience have its full effect, that you may be perfect and complete, lacking in nothing."** I certainly was lacking and I was crying out to God day and night that Carolyn would have a good draw and fill, and that a new kidney would come soon.

Some of our church friends and family knew of our plight. People began to step forward and offer a new kidney. Our hopes would soar only to be dashed when after testing it was learned certain indexes were found to be incompatible. We had to say several times, "Sorry, but we can't accept your kidney." It was moving and heartwarming to see people who were willing to sacrifice a part of themselves for Carolyn. I, myself, did not qualify.

With all of this, God in His mercy knew I was sweating it. On February 16, 2011, during my nap I had a vision. I saw a small clock with hands set at quarter to three. I pondered and prayed about what this meant. We were expecting a big earthquake. I wondered if it meant the earthquake was not far off. But then I remembered it was a small clock. My hopes began to go up. Three is the number of fulfillment and completion. I said to myself, *"The time must be soon for Carolyn to get a transplant."*

On April 5th in the night I saw the same clock but the hands were set at five minutes to three. I started counting: February 16 to April 5 is 48 days, so if ten minutes elapsed in 48 days, then five more minutes would take 24 days. That meant that April 29 ought to be the time. (But as we all know God's timing is seldom our timing.) On April 29th we waited expectantly for a call from San Francisco. None came. It's a good thing it didn't because I was down in my back and Carolyn had a scary crisis of a peritoneal infection. Phil and Anne were standing by to take Carolyn if the call came.

Meanwhile I was carrying a cell phone (first time in my life) so Carolyn could reach me at any time. Wednesday, May 18th, I went to early- morning prayer with Jose, my pastor. I had forgotten my cell phone. Carolyn called via Jose to say San Francisco had called. She was number three in line for a kidney that would be available that day. I went home to wait with Carolyn. David (from UCSF) called three hours later and said Carolyn's stats were a perfect match with a 41-year old kidney. The two others in line before her might not qualify. So he recommended we start out for San Francisco because by the time all the data was in we wouldn't have time to get there.[123] The adrenaline was pumping. Three hours into our drive David called again to give us the glad news that Carolyn was now the number one candidate. We drove to the hospital in 4-1/4 hours (it normally takes five). They rushed to prepare her for 7:00 surgery. I have never witnessed a greater display of teamwork and efficiency in doing all the tests to get her ready. Most important, they had to certify she was free of all infection. At 7:30, three hours after we arrived, they wheeled her into the operating room. She never looked more beautiful. She was at peace. She looked like an angel. Love and prayer were flowing. Tons of people were praying for us. I prayed

---

[123] A kidney can only be kept on ice for a limited period.

all night. The woman surgeon reported to me in the middle of the night that the surgery took three hours; that it was tricky because her new kidney had three major arteries instead of one. Early in the morning I went into Carolyn's room. She was sitting up looking great. She wanted to hold me. She'd been praying and praising all night too. Underneath the bed the prettiest sight I ever saw, a clear bag filling up with urine. I never thought I would praise God for urine.

Carolyn recovered quickly. Much to everyone's surprise, she was discharged three days later.[124] She was in great shape. We were rejoicing with all of our friends, family and intercessors. The only sad part was that we had missed Timothy's wedding (my third grandson married Shelby on May 20th.) We had waited six years. It was worth it. I'll never be impatient again!

Seriously now, I think this is the time to think theologically. In the '60s and '70s I was emphasizing the power of the Holy Spirit in terms of ministry and gifts but I knew all along the fruit of the Spirit – especially patient love – is the most important thing. The great two-fold work of the Spirit is sanctification. It is two-fold because on the one hand the Holy Spirit puts to death in us (mortification) those things that are not like Christ, and on the other hand He brings to life in us (vivification) those things that are truly the character of Christ.

The second half of my life I have spent long hours in the classrooms of patience and kindness and have had incredible long times in the gym to work out (by the delivering grace of God) the terrible sins of anger

---

[124] Have you noticed how many times the word "three" occurs in the last two paragraphs?

and judgment. These times have not been as fun or pleasing as the exciting times of the Spirit's effusion, but they have been very fulfilling. Through it all the Holy Spirit has been an ever-flowing spring.

CHAPTER 32

Fruitful and Multiplying

While Carolyn and I were going through some tough times, my family was blossoming. I had always wanted them to be fruitful and multiply and keep the family together in California. My first grandson Andrew married Charlotte on December 22, 2001 (Dale officiated). Daniel, Emily's second son, married Maria on June 4, 2004 (again Dale officiated). On March 18, 2008, my first great-grandchild Elijah Paulsen was born to Andrew and Charlotte. In the spring of 2008 Casey, my oldest Whitaker grandson asked me if I would perform the marriage for him and Alaina. During the summer of 2008 Carolyn and I had the wonderful privilege of counseling Casey and Alaina to prepare them for marriage. This was a rich time of intimate sharing and then what a thrill it was to officiate at their beautiful wedding at Cypress Ridge on September 27th.

On July 14, 2009, James Paulsen was born to Daniel and Maria. On November 9, 2009, Nathan Paulsen was born to Andrew and Charlotte. On March 27, 2010, Connor (one of Amy and Mike's twins) married

Sherianne. Her pastor officiated and I had a small part in it. Carolyn was so sick and thin she could hardly make it through. On April 22, 2011, Rebekah Paulsen was born to Daniel and Maria and on May 20, 2011, Timothy married Shelby and Dale officiated again. Soon thereafter, as Carolyn recovered from her surgery, we had the delightful privilege of doing premarital counseling with Chad and Ali and then had the joy of officiating at a beautiful big family wedding on August 20th. On December 30th Brendan married Rachel in Michigan and her pastor officiated.

Since then the babies have been multiplying. Aidan McClenahan was born on February 2, 2012 to Connor and Sherianne, Dustin Whitaker was born to Casey and Alaina on July 7, 2012, Bowan McClenahan was born to Connor and Sherianne October 3, 2013, Ashlyn Paulsen was born to Timothy and Shelby April 28, 2013, Levi Whitaker was born to Chad and Ali on April 19, 2014, and Kelsey Whitaker was born to Casey and Alaina on May 31, 2014 and Jane McClenahan was born to Brendan and Rachel on November 18, 2014. Camille Paulsen was born May 15, 2015 to Tim and Shelby. There is one more on the way that we know of as of this writing. Coby Whitaker is engaged to be married later this year and Pat Little is also engaged.

My ancestor, Henry Whitaker, started a new chapter in the history of the Whitaker family when he moved from Bacup, England, to Philadelphia in 1812. I started a new chapter in the Whitaker family when I moved west in 1958. It is amazing to see how God has blessed in the time since. When we gather for our family events with all the in-laws and grandchildren there are 34 of us and, I don't mind saying, they are handsome and beautiful. To God be the praise and the glory.

We are giving thanks and praise to God that all of my children, and grandchildren and spouses are followers of Jesus in the fellowship of the church. All of my great-grandchildren are being raised to love Jesus and follow Him also. I am particularly grateful to say that five of my grandchildren are involved in full or part time church ministries. Andrew has already been ordained as a Youth Pastor and Brendan is preparing for ordination. I'm happy to say that most of my children and grandchildren have experienced the power of the Holy Spirit, and evidence more of the fruit than I did at their ages.

I cannot be complacent. I keep praying that all of us (my whole family) will be continuously "filled with all the fullness of God" (Ephesians 3:19); that we will be radiant witnesses of Jesus Christ, manifesting His goodness, joy and peace. And through us many will come to trust in Jesus to the Glory of God.

I leave you with three quotes that sum up my heart's cry for the future:

1. **"If anyone thirsts, let him come to Me and drink. He who believes in Me, as the scripture has said, 'Out of his heart shall flow rivers of living water.'"** John 7:37-38.
2. "He who prayeth not constantly and diligently for the Spirit of God … is a stranger from Christ and His gospel."[125]
3. "As a foolish church presupposes His (Holy Spirit) presence and action in its own existence … so a

---

[125] Page 155, chapter 2 of John Owen's great work on the Holy Spirit

foolish theology presupposes the Holy Spirit ...
only where the Holy Spirit is sighed, cried, and
prayed for, does He become present and newly
active."[126]

---

[126] Dr. Karl Barth, "The Work of the Holy Spirit," 182 General
Assembly of the United Presbyterian Church.

Hearing God

In living the Christian life, in worship and in service, the all-important thing is sensitivity to the voice of God. It is easy to miss His voice in an indiscriminate following of usual routines or a rigid adherence to traditional styles or even copying another follower of Jesus. On the other hand, it is marvelous to discover His ever-fresh, creative, and surprising ways for our lives and ministries. So then, let us look at some principles of hearing God:

1. The Lord Promises to Guide His Children.

"My sheep hear my voice and I know them and they follow me." John 10:27

"When the Spirit of truth comes, He will guide you into all the truth; for He will not speak on His own authority, but whatever He hears He will speak, and He will declare to you the things that are to come." John 16:13

"If any of you lacks wisdom, let him ask God who gives to all men generously and without reproaching, and it will be given him." James 1:5

2.   Surrender to do the Will of God.

"...if any man's will is to do His will he shall know whether the teaching is from God." John 7:17
"He leads the humble in what is right and teaches the humble His way." Psalm 25:9

First thing every day we need to tell the Lord that whatever the cost, we are ready and willing to obey His voice, and then expect He will guide. Stay humble; don't look for great things, but look for simple, loving ways to serve the Lord and love people.

3.   Cultivate an Inner Quietness that Listens for His voice, and set a regular time daily to meditate on His written Word.

Our lifestyle is drowning out His Word. We need to shut off the computer and TV, avoid a frantic rushed schedule, find a refuge (sometimes the bathroom is the only place), and learn to be "still and know."

The Bible is the most reliable general guide of what He wants us to know, to be, and to do. It is also His best instrument for speaking to us the specific personal Word of application that we need to hear. Take a small portion daily (no more than a paragraph), beginning with the New Testament, and ask Him to speak to you through it. Then read it slowly and reflectively over and over like a love letter, and promise to believe and obey what He says. If we will jot down the lucid impressions that come to us in our daily listening to the Word, then act on them that day, we will find God's Word to us confirmed in action and fruit. Most importantly, we will learn by practice to discern the difference between our thoughts and God's thoughts, and between the impressions of the world, the flesh, the devil, and God. There is no substitute for saturating our whole life with God's written Word; unless we are constantly illuminated by it we will miss God's best. It will keep us from sin and error, it will keep us on the straight and narrow way that leads to heaven, it is complete nourishment for our daily needs, and it is the most effective weapon in the battle of life. God will never speak contrary to the whole truth of Scripture.

4.   Never Ignore Your Conscience.

Your conscience is God's basic word to you. It is normally a reliable guide. It is neither safe nor right to disregard it. Note how much St. Paul emphasizes the importance of obeying conscience. (See Acts 24:16; Romans 2:15, 9:1, 13:5; II Corinthians 1:12, 4:2, 5:11; I Timothy 1:5, 1:19, 3:9; II Timothy 1:3; Titus 1:15.) It is true that conscience is primarily a negative voice, but one of the most saving words I ever heard on guidance was "mind the checks."

5.   Honor Common Sense and Intelligence.

God will not constantly tell us what to do. We are mature sons and daughters of a loving and wise Father who does not want puppets whose every move is controlled by Him. In an early stage of my seeking His will in everything, I often found He was saying, **"Figure it out for yourself."** Most of the time we know what we ought to do -- the good, decent, loving and loyal thing. He has given us minds to use in problem solving. But, having said that, we have tended to "lean unto our own understanding" too much. We have been locked into logical planning and strategizing as our primary way of operating and have shut down on the creative and spontaneous sovereignty of the Spirit.

6.   The Sound of His Voice.

Having observed numbers 1-5 above, we will learn to discern "the still small voice" (I Kings 19:12) of God. It comes through our thoughts – especially as a spontaneous, creative idea that quietly dawns upon us. Or perhaps we should say it comes into our hearts (the Bible often translates "heart" into "mind"), as a gentle prompting or hunch. It is not loud or demanding **("He shall not cry or lift up His voice",** Isaiah 42:2 and Matthew 12:19); we can miss it through inattention or preoccupation with our agenda.

When the little, gentle, quickening comes, it often causes me to have a "Eureka" feeling – it's a neat idea. We may wonder if it's "just me". If it is of God, it will grow on us with a sense of conviction, rightness, peace, and a freedom to act on it. Therefore, we have learned to avoid impulsiveness and to say, "Lord, if this is You, let it grow on me."

Dallas Willard has some very helpful things to say about God's voice. He says that His Word has authority and thus comes with a "certain steady, calm force … inclining us to assent."[127] Certainly this rings true when we remember the impact of Jesus' words as recorded in the Gospels (Matthew 7:29). Personally this "weight of authority" quality is sometimes noted, especially while meditating on the written Word, but

---

[127] "In Search of Guidance," page 188.

the more usual quality noted is: "**The wisdom from above is first pure, then peaceable, gentle, and easy to be entreated, full of mercy and good fruits, without partiality, and without hypocrisy.**" James 3:17.

7.   Suspect words.

It is true that God sometimes speaks in our minds with amazing clarity. The words are direct, authoritative and unforgettable. However, it is good to be cautious of sudden strong impulses, overwhelming emotional flights, overpowering visions, and triumphal imaginations that cater to our pride or selfishness. The devil can manipulate our feelings and run away with our emotions to make fools of us and discredit the work of God. We should never act on a strong experience or vision or prophecy until we have sifted it through patient prayer and it is confirmed through a growing sense of righteousness, joy, and peace (Romans 14:17).

<u>Ordinary</u> inspiration is the surest; the gentle inclination of love, mercy, and truth grows on us with conviction and cannot be counterfeited by Satan. In Philippians 2:13, God promises to work in us **"to will ... for His good pleasure."** As a result, His commands come to us as good desires springing up within like a light rising within. Jeremiah 31:33 says that He writes His laws on our hearts so that we desire to do what we ought. We are <u>drawn</u> rather than driven.

8.   Move in Humble Faith.

If we think we are being prompted of God along the lines described in #6, then we should begin to move in faith to obey. We might say, "I'm not sure about this, but I think the Lord wants me to do such and such." Elbert Hubbard said, "Go as far as you can see and when you get there you'll see further."

9. Circumstances Open Up.

When God speaks, circumstances will tend to confirm it providing we act in a right spirit of humility, love and truth. A door opens; a means is provided; or despite obstacles we are given unusual faith, vision and energy with which to surmount the obstacles. All of nature and humanity is God's servant and so they cooperate or seem favorable. **"Light rises in the darkness for the upright."** Psalm 112:4

10. Confirmation through Counsel.

If we are unsure, we are wise to seek Godly counsel. **"In the multitude of counselors there is safety."** Psalm 11:4. Feedback and evaluations by objective, mature Christians are invaluable helps. Often God confirms through our spouse, best friends, or pastor.

11. Remember.

We are sheep of the Good Shepherd. He leads gently like a shepherd. He is never in a rush, nor is He impulsive, rude or irritating. He treats us with the utmost respect and courtesy and kindness. On the other hand, Satan pushes, shoves, agitates, and makes frantic; he manipulates with fear and guilt; he is like a bee in a bottle; he harasses with confusion and he has no time to wait.

12.   The Acid Test.

When in doubt, pray. If it's God, you will be more and more at peace about it. **"The effect of righteousness will be peace."** Isaiah 32:17. **"Let the peace of Christ rule in your hearts."** Colossians 3:15. If it's not God, you become more and more uneasy about it. **"There will be tribulation and anguish for every human being who does evil**." Romans 2:9.

Dennis Bennett

When I met Dennis at the Seattle airport, I was struck by how handsome and youthful he was. Actually he was 46. I found him to be a man of culture and learning with a boyish heart. He had a childlike simplicity and directness and the faith of Abraham coupled with charm and love. He was bold, intense, a very hard worker and a faithful pastor to his people. He was bright and very gifted. He played the piano and the guitar very well and he was a licensed pilot. He and Elberta had four grown children when I visited them. Elberta was a slender and gracious woman. She walked and conducted herself like a queen. Unless I had been told, I would not have known that she was seriously ill with cancer. She cooked me two meals and the two of them took me to dinner on several occasions, but she never said anything about her illness. Later that year she died and, of course, it was a great loss to Dennis, his children, and St. Luke's.

While I was in Seattle, Dennis had me with him most of the time so I could see and hear what really goes on in a Spirit-filled church. The one thing I couldn't get over was the attendance at a Thursday morning communion and healing service. The small church was full (probably about 100 people). I have never felt a stronger sense of the presence of God. My feeling was, these people have not come to get something so much as they have come to pour out what God had been pouring in all week. The Episcopal liturgy enabled the praises and prayers of the people. I had never seen a liturgical service that seemed to flow as this one did. There was form and procedure, but immense freedom and joy. After the communion, which was beautifully done, people were invited to the altar to receive prayer for healing and I was invited to help minister to people as though I was one of their own leaders.

I visited St. Luke's and Dennis on several other occasions when I was in Seattle on preaching missions for the Presbyterians. I saw the parish grow to be one of the strongest churches in the whole northwest and to be a center of spiritual renewal worldwide.

Throughout the '60s and '70s, Dennis definitely was one of the most prominent spearheads for the Charismatic movement, both in the Episcopal church and in ecumenical gatherings in the United States and worldwide. After Elberta's death he married Rita Reed and the two of them ministered together, especially in the United States, and wrote many books concerning the work of the Holy Spirit. Our fellowship was often renewed because we would end up in the same conferences or minister's meetings somewhere in the United States. At a minister's retreat at Oral Roberts University, he was my roommate and he also came to conduct our staff retreat when I was in Glendale. Even with all he had to do, he wrote to me periodically, especially in times of crisis, and his counsel was always wise and brave.

APPENDIX C

The Story of the Murphree Child

Early in my ministry at Chandler I married a charming young couple, Pat and Pennee Murphree. We became close friends. They soon had two children, Brent and Julie. Then in October 1963 little Jill was born premature. She was immediately placed in an oxygen tent and was not expected to live. In my newfound zeal for healing I encouraged the Murphrees to believe God would heal Jill and mobilized prayer on her behalf. I think I even assured Pat and Pennee the Lord would heal her.

I went to the hospital and baptized the child by reaching my wet palm into the incubator and placing it upon her head and praying a most urgent prayer. Soon thereafter Jill died. It was naturally an awful blow. I tried to comfort the parents.

Within a few weeks Pat came to see me in my office. I can still see him standing there in his Levis and his western hat. He was an intelligent progressive farmer. He said, "Bob, you gotta face it, all this talk about God

215

healing is a bunch of stuff. We've had it and we're done with it, and we're not coming to church," and then he left.

I was thunderstruck and in grief. They were a favorite couple and I had ruined their faith. I fell on my couch and poured out my heart to God, *"What am I going to do?"* I desperately wanted to do something to make it right. I was in agony. Before long the Lord impressed upon me I was just to pray for them and wait for Him to work.

Before many weeks Pat was back. He told me, "I don't understand what's happening. We feel different. I'm sorry I said the things I said. Something new is happening in us. We are more hopeful and believing. We want to get our friends to come over to the house and we want you to come and lead us in Bible study." (Inside of me I was shouting, *"Hallelujah. God you're so good, I can't believe this is happening. Glory to You Lord."*)

So we started to gather with a number of young couples in the little Murphree farmhouse in Higley. God gave me grace to begin with Genesis and go through the scriptures and nourish these young people on the wonderful Word of Life. That was the start of a new young adult group that kindled a number of people in vital faith and a dynamic awareness of the presence of God. Eventually the group was too big for the Murphree home and we went to the Rowe home.

Later on when a woman in my church circulated a scandalous letter charging me with being a false prophet and a wolf in sheep's clothing, Pat and Pennee and their friends were among my chief defenders.

Their daughter Julie was frequently sick. Pat and Pennee often called me to come and pray for her. She struggled with chest diseases and asthma. She was sick so much she had to be hospitalized a number of times. In my entire ministry I believe that of necessity she was the child I prayed for the most. The Murphrees kept on believing even though her health continued to be precarious until she was in her mid-teens. Then through surgery for a hiatal hernia she was put on the road to health. She grew up to be one of the strongest and consistent witnesses I have ever known.

Whenever I teach on healing I usually deal with the question, "What do we do when the prayer of faith is seemingly not answered? What do we say to the people whose faith is undermined by the apparent failure?" I answer those questions with the Jill story and with Corrie's words, "Jesus brings life out of suffering and death."

APPENDIX D

Corrie ten Boom

After the devastation of WWII, millions of people in Europe were looking for long-lost loved ones. In their desperation, many went to fortunetellers or mediums to help locate their loved ones. Then they wondered why darkness came into their spiritual lives. Corrie would point to the scriptures, such as Leviticus 19:31 and 20:27, Deut. 18:9-12, which warn people to stay away from psychics – because it is idolatry and leads to death. Then she would lead them to confess that they had sinned against God, ask forgiveness and invite Jesus to cleanse them of this sin through His blood and to be their Savior and Lord.

In subsequent years, she would run into others who admitted going to psychics who would say to her, "I didn't know it was a sin, I was just curious and having fun." In response, she would tell this story:

"Some boys were playing ball in West Germany near the border of East Germany. Unfortunately a ball flew over to East Germany, which was separated from the West by a barbed wire fence. One boy decided he would crawl through the barbed wire and retrieve the ball despite the warning signs. The Communist police grabbed him. Startled by this seizure, the boy said, 'I was just playing. I meant no harm.' Their response was, 'Too bad, you have trespassed and you must go to jail.'" Corrie would say, "When you go into enemy territory, there are deadly consequences."

Corrie ten Boom never went to college; she was a watchmaker like her father, yet she was far more effective than most as a preacher and counselor. She always gave the credit to Jesus, but it needs to be said that it also came from godly parents who dearly loved and taught Corrie and her two sisters and brother. The parents modeled selflessness and trust; they always took in people who needed a home. First there were elderly aunts, then foster children, then Jews who were being hunted by the Nazis. Corrie eventually took the lead in this merciful household. It became part of the Dutch underground resistance movement and that meant increasing danger and intrigue. The ten Booms knew eventually they would be caught and pay dearly, but they did it out of faithfulness to God. When they were raided in February 1944 and put in prison, Corrie's mother was already deceased; her older brother and sister lived elsewhere, but her elderly father died within ten days of his imprisonment. Corrie and her (7 years older) sister Betsy ended up in Ravensbruck concentration camp (Germany). After much hard labor, cruelty and starvation rations, Betsy died, but not before she and Corrie ministered the Word of Life to many in the cramped, lice-ridden barracks.

Corrie, describing what God did, quoted Romans 8:35-37: **"Who shall separate us from the love of Christ? Shall tribulation, or distress, or** persecution, or famine, or nakedness, or peril, or sword? .... No, in all these things, we are more than conquerors through Him that loved us." "It was not a wish. It was a fact. We knew it; we experienced it minute-by-minute – poor, hated, hungry. 'We are more than conquerors,' not, 'we shall be.' We are! Life in Ravensbruck took place on two separate levels, mutually impossible. One, the observable, external life, grew every day more horrible. The other, the life we lived with God, grew daily better, truth upon truth, glory upon glory."[128] The glory increased after Ravensbruck – Corrie forgave the man who betrayed her family to the Gestapo, plus those who killed her father, sister and nephew. Then she opened her home to care for the despised Dutch collaborators.

Corrie, and her helper Conny, told me that Chandler Presbyterian Church was their favorite place to come in America, because they sensed the tremendous prayer support and felt ministered to as well as being ministers. She said in her newsletter,[129] "Never before have I experienced such a working of the Holy Spirit, such a teamwork with the children of God and seen so many miracles. People were liberated from demons of fear, alcoholism, and others. Sick people were healed, sinners trusted the Lord for salvation, and Christians received a new vision of the victorious life. Many surrendered themselves to the Lord and were filled with the Holy Spirit."

Later, in 1972, I arranged for her to preach at Glendale Presbyterian Church, where she also packed them in. In the early '80s she could travel no more.

---

[128] "The Hiding Place" by Corrie ten Boom, page 178.
[129] "It's Harvest Time," December 1963-January/February 1964.

She was mostly confined to bed in a friend's home in Placentia, California. I went with Peter Marshall, Jr. to pray with her. She was still spending her days praying for visitors, showing them the way of salvation and autographing her books for them. Within a year of our visit, Corrie died April 16, 1983 at the age of 91. I still have her copy of "The Hiding Place," with her favorite autograph, "At our side is a Mighty High Priest and legions of angels. Halleluja."

APPENDIX E

Story of Dr. John Mackay[130]

In the spring of 1967 when I saw that I was likely to be in trouble with the leadership of my Presbytery and denomination, I wrote to Dr. John Mackay. Brick had told me that since he had been a missionary to Peru in his early years, he had become a friend and advocate of the Pentecostal movement. As the President of Princeton Seminary, and as a prestigious leader in the ecumenical movement, he was the one who in the 1950s opened the door for David duPlessis to speak to the leaders and ministers of the mainline Protestant churches.

I told Dr. Mackay about myself and my ministry and the situation with my church and the Presbytery Commission. I shared in full my witness and my charismatic convictions, and asked him to be a counselor and advocate for me. Dr. Mackay responded warmly and encouragingly. He assured me that he believed that what I had was of God and my effort to

---

[130] The full story of Dr. Mackay's role is told in, *American Presbyterians, Journal of Presbyterian History,* Volume 72, Number 3, Fall 1994, page 141.

bring about Holy Spirit renewal in the church was a good cause. He asked that I keep him fully informed and he would work at the highest levels of the church to make sure that my cause would receive a considered hearing and that the church would eventually be open to the truth that I represented.

I continued to correspond with Dr. Mackay throughout 1967 and the first half of 1968. I still have at least seven of his letters to me and they were always signed, "Affectionately, John A. Mackay." While I was meeting with the Commission, he was meeting with some of the distinguished leaders of the Presbyterian Church to share with them what I, and scores of other charismatic Presbyterian ministers, was going through in our respective situations. When the Presbytery of Phoenix ousted me, he shared my story with the Stated Clerk of the denomination, Dr. Wm. Thompson, who assured Dr. Mackay that the General Assembly would appoint a commission to deal with the theological and biblical issues. Mackay relayed to me that Thompson was personally distressed by what the Phoenix Presbytery did. Later, when the Special Committee on the Work of the Holy Spirit was appointed, Dr. Mackay had suggested half of the people, and the Chairman was the man who sat next to me at General Assembly, Dr. John Strock. All along, Dr. Mackay encouraged me by saying that when my case came to trial the Lord of the Church would be with me and he was convinced the Church would not let me down. Though he never told me, I know in my heart that he personally spoke to some of the judges to assure them that my cause was just and I was a sincere person who deserved a fair hearing. Not only that, but the Moderator in 1967, Dr.

Eugene Smathers, was an old friend of mine who had been a neighboring pastor in Tennessee and knew me well. I am persuaded that he, also, put in a good word for me with the judges.

Dr. Mackay also went the second mile for me. He talked on several occasions with my father who had been a Princeton University man. My father was most concerned about what I was going through and gave me wonderful advice. Mackay was encouraging to him also and told him of his esteem for me and how he was working to make sure that I would be sustained and that my cause would triumph. You can imagine what that meant to my parents.

APPENDIX F

Catholic-Pentecostal Dialogue

The outcome of our meeting with the Secretariat for the Promotion of Christian Unity was that a permanent dialogue was set up to begin in 1972[131]. It was agreed that nine Pentecostal/Charismatic representatives and seven Roman Catholic representatives would meet annually for five years. The purpose was to foster the coming together of Christians in prayer and common witness and to build a united testimony concerning the fullness of life in the Holy Spirit. There was no intention of seeking to establish structural unity between the churches. It was determined that the meetings would center around academic and theological papers that addressed such matters as Baptism in the Holy Spirit, the giving of the Spirit and Christian initiation, and the meaning of Charismatic Renewal for the churches. The

---

[131] It was an honor to be invited to be part of the dialogue, but instead I nominated my friend Dr. J. Rodman Williams to go in my place. I did that because he was much brighter and was already a distinguished theologian of the Charismatic Movement. He was also a gracious gentleman. He had a most enlightening affect on the dialogues.

participants also prayed and fellowshipped together over a period of four days each year.

The initial five dialogues were so successful in terms of building friendships and exchanging understanding that the dialogues continued throughout the '70s and continue to this day (2015). It has meant that a growing number of distinguished Pentecostal and Catholic scholars and leaders have come to know each other at a deep level which, in turn, has influenced their respective constituencies with a greater love for one another and a deeper fellowship in the Holy Spirit. They have demonstrated what Dr. John Mackay long ago forecast when he said, "The future of the Christian movement may well belong to a renewed Catholicism and a matured Pentecostalism.

I am happy to say that after one year of the new Pope Francis it is public knowledge that he is openly charismatic. Bishop Tony Palmer, a long-time friend of Pope Francis, at a meeting in Texas in early 2014, publicly stated this.[132] This is not surprising since several of his recent predecessors in the Papacy gave strong encouragement to the charismatic movement in the Catholic Church.

---

[132] "Pope Francis talks about unity with Kenneth Copeland" YouTube 45-minute version.

APPENDIX G

Prayer for Healing of Plants & Trees

When we feel so led to pray for a sick plant or tree, we will touch the plant and say something like, *"In the Name of the Lord Jesus Christ we bless you. We take authority over every sickness, infection, and disease and command you to go and stay away."* We may do this several times for a tree with the laying on of hands depending on how we are guided. Basically we pray a prayer of authority. Historically Christian leaders have prayed in this way for crops and for herds. We also will pray that God will guide us as to any natural measures we should take to help the plant prosper. In the case of our trees at Tahoe, even though the Forrester did not advise it, we watered our trees during the hot period.

APPENDIX H

Len LeSourd & Catherine Marshall

I loved and admired Len LeSourd and Catherine Marshall. I had come to know them in the early days of the outpouring of the Holy Spirit. When I was put out of my church at Chandler, Catherine Marshall was one of the first to write me a letter of encouragement and to offer help and included a generous check. She said at the time, "I believe our paths are destined to cross." How true that was. Before long we were meeting each other at regional conferences of the PCC.

Her husband, Len, whom she married in 1949, was one of the early leaders of our fellowship and served on the Board several times with me. He was like an older brother. I admired him because he had been a fighter pilot in Europe in World War II and was a great tennis player. He was handsome and easygoing and terrifically able as a writer and an editor. He was the head of Guide Post magazine for twenty-five years and started Chosen Books. The first book he wrote under the Chosen label was "Born Again" about Chuck

Colson. It was a huge success. I loved working with him. He encouraged me in my writing and gave me lots of insights. It was his intention to write a book about Sam after he grew up.

We had Catherine as a featured speaker for a huge national PCC meeting where we packed out the Pasadena Center (there were also a number of other great speakers). I really felt Catherine was prophetic. She wrote a book in 1961 titled, "Beyond Ourselves," which helped to instigate the whole move of the Holy Spirit in the world. Then again, she wrote an even more powerful book in 1974 titled, "Something More," which gave a fresh impetus to the movement and also very valuable teaching. When she died in 1983 she had sold over 16,000,000 books she had written or edited and was the number one religious all-time best seller. We thought alike in many ways and I was involved in prayer covenants with her for several years about crucial matters. Marilyn and I also became good friends with her son, Peter Marshall Jr. and his wife Edith.

Catherine was very interested in my crisis of faith in seminary and how God led me to deal with it. It reminded her of her father's experience. She interviewed me about it at length and incorporated it in her book about the Johnstown flood.

APPENDIX I

How to Meditate on the Word

In Christian meditation we are not studying scripture, but listening for God to speak to us through His word. Here are some important directives.

1. Have a regular time to listen to God; put everything else second.
2. Remove distractions: turn off the phone, get alone in a quiet place; have a "things to do" list so that when concerns come you can write them down to deal with later.
3. Relax: get comfortable; breathe slowly and deeply, ask the Lord to help you, **"Be still and know that I am God."** Gently turn over to Him anxieties, pressures, distractions.
4. As you prepare to turn to scripture, ask the Lord to speak to you through the passage and make the truth a living reality within you.

To begin with, take the Gospel of Mark.[133] Focus on one paragraph or scene each day. Read the Word like

---

[133] Eventually go through all four gospels.

a love letter from the Lord to you; savor each word and phrase. Read it slowly and reflectively.

Close your eyes and picture the whole scene as vividly as possible. See yourself as part of the scene; preferably you are the person who is ministered to (the leper or the paralytic) or be one of the disciples watching. Picture Jesus speaking and acting toward you in saving love and grace. Get into the whole scene imaginatively – let your whole mind and spirit be flooded with His presence. Ask Him what He wants you to know, i.e. His promise and His goodness, and what He wants you to do, i.e. trusting Him more and obeying His word.

If you take fifteen minutes a day to live in the scripture with your imagination, your mind will be renewed. The redemptive scenes of the gospels will gradually push out the lustful images of the past. This type of meditation played a big part in Christian history. It was beloved by the great saints. **"And we all, with unveiled face, beholding the glory of the Lord, are being changed into His likeness from one degree of glory to another."** 2 Corinthians 3:18.

Following our time in the Word it is important to record what was experienced, what the Lord impressed upon us, and what we are going to do about it.

APPENDIX J

The Biblical Teaching on Homosexuality

"Throughout the Old Testament, sexual expression is presented as a gift and blessing of God within the institution of marriage between the sexes. The loneliness of man is remedied by the creation of woman, and their union of compassion and procreation is established within the context of the family. Fornication, adultery and homosexuality are condemned as deviations from this pattern. Sexual expression outside the covenant of heterosexual marriage is depicted as dangerous to the social order and symbolic of the spiritual adultery involved in idolatrous worship."[134] (Genesis 1 and 2)

"Leviticus 18:22 and 20:13 forbid male homosexual behavior in a context which includes condemnation of incest, adultery, bestiality, and the sacrifice of children to Molech, prescribing the death penalty in each case. Genesis 19:1-29 describes the judgment of God in the destruction of Sodom and Gomorrah...the decadence

---

[134] The passages in quotations are from Dr. Richard F. Loveless in "Healing for the Homosexual."

of Sodom was proverbial; homosexual immorality was one important element in that decadence."

"In Matthew 19:1-12, Jesus reaffirms the Old Testament teaching that sexual expression is to be channeled within the covenant of heterosexual marriage. He commends the alternative of celibacy to those who do not marry." Though Jesus never mentioned homosexuality by name, He was tougher on adultery and divorce than Moses was. (See Matthew 5:27-32 and 19:1-9.) The Jews considered any sexual relationship other than heterosexual marriage as adultery. This is true in Christian history also.

Jesus' disciples uniformly condemned fornication, adultery, incest and homosexual practice. (See Romans 1:24-27, 1 Corinthians 6:9-10, 1 Timothy 1:8-10, 2 Peter 2:6-10 and Jude 7.) In Romans Paul describes homosexual desire among women as well as men as "dishonorable." He also called homosexual behavior "against nature." 1 Corinthians 6:9-10 indicates that those who persistently and unrepentedly go on in the practice of homosexuality will not inherit the Kingdom of God, along with unrepentant fornicators, idolaters, adulterers, thieves, the covetous, drunkards, revilers and swindlers.

Paul's teaching that homosexual behavior is against nature deserves reflection. Obviously the male genitals fit with the female, and they naturally yield fruit (children). Anal intercourse (sodomy) is unnatural; as a result it often leads to a deformed rectum, serious disease (not only AIDS) and early death. Further, this sinful practice leads to spiritual death and despair and no natural fruit. God calls it an "abomination" (Leviticus 18:22, 20:13; Deut. 7:25).

Now I must say some solemn words. Our society is under judgment; it has been for some time. One of the signs of God's displeasure with us is the crazy and destructive weather (drought, fire, floods, hurricanes, tornadoes, earthquakes, etc.). In the Old Testament, sodomy brought down a terrible fiery calamity upon Sodom and Gomorrah. Could it be that as people increasingly accept and embrace abominable sexual behavior, which is against nature, now nature has turned against us? (I realize that is not the only reason for nature to turn against us; the killing of 50,000,000 babies through abortion is undoubtedly another major reason.)

APPENDIX K

Pastor Larry Christenson

I had known Larry since we moved to Glendale. I visited him at his Holy Trinity Lutheran Church on a residential hill overlooking the harbor at San Pedro, California. I wanted to know him since he was already one of the bright young leaders of the charismatic renewal because of his little booklet, "Speaking in Tongues, A Gift for the Body of Christ." (The first of many books.) I found him to be a very well disciplined and trustworthy person. He had been a Phi Beta Kappa student and was a few years older than I and had received the Baptism of the Holy Spirit a year before I had.

We began to meet together for sharing and prayer and before long we began to reach out to other denominational friends who had had a charismatic experience. Our times of prayer were wonderfully inspirational and supportive as we found our way in denominations that were leery of our experience. In the course of time we invited Father Ralph Tichenor, SJ, from Loyola University, the head of the Catholic charismatic renewal group to join us and slowly the group grew. Eventually we were meeting about every six weeks throughout the '70s and had an attendance of 15-20 men. Larry's assistant, Paul Anderson, also became part of our group and led us in marvelous worship.

In some ways I envied Larry. It appeared to me that his church was perfectly run; everything was well done. Everybody seemed to have a responsibility and carried it out in harmony with everyone else and the church was a model family. They even had their own Christian school for their children grades 1-12. Larry's messages were well planned and thoughtfully given with a good sense of humor. He was invited to be one of the main speakers at most of the major national and international renewal conferences in those days. In 1983 he became the Director of the International Lutheran Renewal Center in St. Paul, Minnesota. I felt like it was the ultimate compliment when he invited me to do a preaching mission at his church and also when I was asked to be the speaker at their church retreat in the San Bernardino Mountains.

During the '70s tensions developed between national charismatic leaders. There was the main body of the movement and there was a segment of the movement that emphasized a type of mentorship that required people to be strongly submitted to their pastoral mentors and leaders. This became a problem when some ministries felt that other ministries were stealing their sheep and causing them to lose their Christian freedom through an over emphasis on submission. In our national leaders meetings no one was more important and strategic in bringing about understanding between these two groups than Larry.

He was able to do so because he was well related with all parties and had their trust. He was always even-steven and had a gift of wisdom and prophetic insight, which gave wonderful stability to the movement.

APPENDIX L

Obituary

MARILYN ELLIS WHITAKER
JULY 1, 1930 – NOVEMBER 7, 1997

Marilyn Ellis Whitaker died Friday night, November 7th, at her home in Arroyo Grande, California, after a thirteen-year battle with cancer. Marilyn was born July 1, 1930 in Philadelphia, Pennsylvania of Pennsylvania Dutch and Scotch-Irish parents.

"Lynn" grew up in Glenside, PA, and was distinguished as a student, athlete, cheerleader, and delightful friend. She graduated from Cheltenham High and Drexel University. In 1951 Marilyn discovered Christ as her Savior and Lord and soon thereafter taught Home Economics and English at a Mission High School in Albuquerque, NM.

In 1953, she married her childhood friend, Robert Whitaker, and taught High School English and Home Economics in New Haven, CT, in order to help put her husband through seminary at Yale Divinity School.

Through a succession of church pastorates, including First Presbyterian Church of Allardt, First Presbyterian Church of Chandler, Glendale Presbyterian Church and

Silverlake Presbyterian Church, she thought of herself as a "helpmate" to her pastor husband. She always taught Sunday School to little children, led Women's Fellowships, became a Deacon, gave sacrificially to the needy, consistently gave to schools and the community her time and leadership in PTA and other organizations, and modeled the humility and grace of Jesus.

Marilyn was a creative homemaker – gifted in art and music, cooking, crafts, and tailoring. She made her home a haven for kids needing love. She had five children and ten grandchildren.

Marilyn is remembered as a totally giving and caring person. She served with joy and is known for her humor and winsome ways.

Marilyn is survived by her husband, Reverend Robert C. Whitaker; a sister, Winnie; a brother, Robert; children Emily Paulsen of Morro Bay, CA; Laura Little of La Junta, CO; Philip Whitaker of Arroyo Grande, CA; Amy McClenahan of Moraga, CA; and Sam Whitaker of Montrose, CA. Grandchildren include Andrew, Daniel and Timothy Paulsen; Patrick & Shannon Little; Casey, Chad & Coby Whitaker; and Brendan & Connor McClenahan.

APPENDIX M

Symptoms or Signs of Sexual Molestation

It is estimated that one out of every four or five American girls are sexually molested in early childhood or teenage years. It is usually done by a close relative such as the father, brother, or grandfather. (This is the sin of incest, which the Bible roundly condemns.) Molestation causes serious emotional scarring for any child to whom it happens. It also happens to boys. Some of the symptoms are as follows:

1. Low self-esteem; body neglect or over attention to the body.
2. Involvement in abusive relationships.
3. Difficulty in sleeping. Events repeated in dreams relate to age of molestation.
4. The person cannot remember certain years and/ or certain places in their childhood homes.
5. Depression.
6. Exaggerated need to please.

7. Under or overly interested in sex as a child.
8. Sexual promiscuity, and possible homosexual fantasies.
9. Addiction to drugs and/or alcohol is likely.
10. Eating disorders. Anorexia nervosa, bulimia and obesity are very common.
11. Women who have been incested are likely to have difficulty being sexually intimate with their husbands and frequently are frigid.
12. The person often has multiple marriages.
13. High tolerance to pain.
14. Blind to the faults of the perpetrator.

A person may have been molested in childhood or even youth and because of <u>repression</u> have no memory of such things taking place. The above symptoms are clues that <u>perhaps</u> abuse did take place. If you have or had all or most of these symptoms, you ought to pray and ask the Lord to reveal to you if indeed you were molested. He can do this through dreams or visions or the recall of memories. We ought not to dig for these memories, but simply lay it before the Lord as a concern and trust that if there is something we need to know, He will reveal it in His own good time. If and when it is revealed, you need to go to somebody experienced in praying for victims of sexual molestation and have them pray for the healing of memories and liberation from the affects.

Great caution needs to be exercised in coming to the conclusion that you, or the person you are praying for, have been molested and suspecting a certain perpetrator. There is a well-known phenomenon called "false memory syndrome." Many people have falsely accused members of their family for molestation and caused great trouble. Accusation is a very serious sin. Even if we are sure of the guilt of someone, we need to be very careful in whom we confide.

To contact the author
Email: <u>twowhitakers@gmail.com</u>

Made in the USA
Middletown, DE
15 July 2022